Amazing Grace

Amazing Grace

A CULTURAL HISTORY OF THE BELOVED HYMN

James Walvin

UNIVERSITY OF CALIFORNIA PRESS

University of California Press
Oakland, California

© 2023 by James Walvin

Cataloging-in-Publication data is on file at the Library of Congress.

ISBN 978-0-520-39182-6 (cloth : alk. paper)
ISBN 978-0-520-39183-3 (ebook)

Manufactured in the United States of America

32   31   30   29   28   27   26   25   24
10   9   8   7   6   5   4   3   2

publication supported by a grant from
The Community Foundation for Greater New Haven
as part of the **Urban Haven Project**

To the loving memory of my grandparents, Carrie and Robert Wood, who sustained us in hard times

Amazing grace, how sweet the sound
That saved a wretch like me
I once was lost, but now am found
Was blind, but now I see

'Twas grace that taught my heart to fear
And grace my fears relieved
How precious did that grace appear
The hour I first believed

Through many dangers, toils, and snares
We have already come
'Twas grace has brought us safe thus far
And grace will lead us home

When we've been there ten thousand years
Bright, shining as the sun
We've no less days to sing God's praise
Than when we've first begun

Amazing grace, how sweet the sound
That saved a wretch like me
I once was lost, but now am found
Was blind, but now I see

CONTENTS

ILLUSTRATIONS

Introduction

THE WORDS AND MUSIC of "Amazing Grace" are well known to millions of people the world over. Though the words were written in the late eighteenth century, and the music evolved in the nineteenth century (though with much older origins), the hymn's modern popularity emerged quite suddenly after 1970 and has endured for the past fifty years. From 1970 onwards, the hymn has enjoyed remarkable commercial success. It has sold millions of records, as singles, on 45s and on LPs, and more recently on video and digital recordings. It has been recorded by innumerable artists: by major singers and musicians, by orchestras, bands, and pipers. It has appeared in every conceivable genre of music, from rap to classical renditions, and has been recorded in some of the world's great concert halls, in South African townships, in churches, on windswept coastal promontories, and in many hundreds of private homes, thanks to the astonishing technology available in the modern digital age. Any number of professional singers and musicians have adopted "Amazing Grace" as their own theme song. In the process, "Amazing Grace" has transformed some performers into global superstars and has helped fill the coffers of major entertainment corporations.

In addition, and especially over the course of the past half century, "Amazing Grace" has moved far beyond the lucrative, eye-catching world of commercial music-making to establish itself as a simple hymn for humankind. It is at once Christian in origin and expression, yet widely loved because of its simple secular appeal. "Amazing Grace" has become a source of support for individuals, and sometimes whole nations, in times of trouble and distress. Above all perhaps, it has also become a ready-made musical tribute and comfort, played in the shadow of grief and bereavement. Today all this is well known, but it is much less clear how it came to be.

How did "Amazing Grace" come to occupy such an unusual—perhaps even unique—position? How did a hymn written by an English cleric in the late eighteenth century become so important in the lives of millions of people in the twenty-first? What is the trajectory of the hymn as it emerged from its conception in eighteenth-century England to its current position of widespread affection? Equally curious, John Newton, the man who wrote "Amazing Grace," had, in his early years, been the captain of a slave ship. Here was a man involved in the grim cruelties of buying and transporting Africans across the Atlantic. Yet twenty years after he left his slave ship in Liverpool, he wrote a hymn that is widely loved by African Americans—descendants of those enslaved people—and by millions of others for the way it speaks to compassion and salvation, qualities Newton never showed to the ranks of Africans packed onboard his ships.

Many people may be perplexed by John Newton. He is remembered primarily for his godly work and for his uplifting hymns, though his earlier life was marked by inhuman brutality. What enabled a man with such a violent background to write a hymn of enduring compassion and hope? How could a man whose slaving days were marked by callous brutality become so devout, so godly, and so influential a Christian?

We need to remember that John Newton was not alone. Indeed in many respects he was typical of his contemporaries. There was nothing unusual in finding eighteenth-century God-fearing people involved in the godless business of slavery and slave trading. On both sides of the Atlantic there were countless white merchants, politicians, royals, sailors, landowners, planters—and even clerics—who saw no conflict between their involvement with Atlantic slavery and their religion. Moreover, few of Newton's contemporaries thought there was a clash between their Christian faith and their cruelty towards enslaved Africans.[1] We ought not to be surprised that a man of God had been a slaver. Long before Newton, the Christian world had sanctioned the enslavement of Africans. From the earliest days of American settlement, when Bartolomé de Las Casas, bishop of Chiapas, formally called "Defender of the Indians," specifically sanctioned African slavery in Spanish America, very few clerics, congregations, and individual Christians felt any qualms about African enslavement—though Las Casas himself came to regret his initial support for it. Throughout colonial North America, particularly in the US South in the run-up to the Civil War, there were lively theological justifications for slavery.[2] The harsh reality remains: John Newton belonged to a Western Christian culture in which, until very late in the day, only a tiny fraction of white believers saw any moral or religious objection to slavery. He was just one small element in a society where the buying, selling, and owning of Africans went largely unchallenged. Though it may surprise us today, vanishingly few of his white contemporaries ever thought about it.

It is true however that John Newton changed, and so too did many others. The preacher who wrote "Amazing Grace" in 1772 was not the same man who captained the Liverpool slave ship *Duke of Argyle* in 1750. Moreover, Newton spent much of his later life confessing the wickedness of his earlier years, praying for forgiveness, and seeking, as best he could, to redeem himself. After 1787 he finally broke cover, turned against slavery in public, and lent his powerful voice to the campaign by the British Society for Effecting the Abolition of the Slave Trade to bring the slave trade to an end. That trade was abolished by the British Parliament in 1807—the year of Newton's death.

Whichever way we view John Newton, his most astonishing memorial remains his hymn, "Amazing Grace," which continues to have a humane resonance 250 years after he wrote it. How can we explain the appeal and relevance for millions of people in 2022 of a hymn that was written specifically for humble rural parishioners of an isolated English village in 1772? This book is an attempt to offer an explanation.

. . .

My first serious encounter with "Amazing Grace" was not in church but in my work on slavery and the slave trade. John Newton the slave ship captain and author of "Amazing Grace" has drifted in and out of a number of my earlier books on slavery. In places I devoted a great deal of attention to him. Almost inevitably, "Amazing Grace" became, after a fashion, a musical background to much of what I wrote.[3] At the same time I also developed a highly personal curiosity about the hymn. As a schoolboy, I had belonged to the choir at St. John's Church in Failsworth, Greater Manchester, and eventually became head choirboy. Between 1948 when I joined the choir and 1960 when I abandoned the church, I adhered to a regime of choral singing, with weekly rehearsals and two, sometimes three, services every Sunday, in addition to all the other high days of the Christian calendar. Not surprisingly, my head soon filled with dozens of the hymns that I sang every week. To this day, I know many of them by heart, and though I lost my faith more than six decades ago, I still enjoy singing those hymns (though normally my only opportunity to do so takes place at funerals). But among the many hymns which those years of youthful choral singing implanted in my brain, "Amazing Grace" is notable for its absence. It did not appear in the hymnbook used in my church, and it continues to be absent from many of the subsequent editions published for the Church of England. As a result, I came late to the pleasures and the curiosities of "Amazing Grace," and I did so, not in England where I live, but on my frequent visits to the US, when teaching and researching the history of slavery.

The ubiquity of "Amazing Grace" in modern American cultural life, indeed the way it often seems to provide a soundtrack to American life itself, left me curious. What is so special about "Amazing Grace"? Its appeal can't merely be the simple music, nor even its memorable verses. After all, there are many other hymns which are no less impressive, and which have equally haunting music. Why "Amazing Grace"? How did the words of an English slave trader develop such a unique status and position in American life—and far beyond the US? This simple curiosity took on a greater urgency when it was fired by one particular event.

In 2015 President Obama sang "Amazing Grace" at a funeral in Charleston. It was a breathtaking moment of political brilliance and a unique historical moment. The reaction of Obama's audience that day in

Charleston was equally revealing. What was it about that hymn, that president, that congregation, in that city, that seemed to speak to a much more complex and tangled story of the US and of its tortured, slavery-based history? I set out to explore that story.

. . .

In June 2015, a white supremacist gunman shot dead the Reverend Clementa Pinckney, a South Carolina state senator and charismatic pastor, along with eight of his parishioners, as they gathered for a Bible reading session in their Charleston church, Emanuel African Methodist Episcopal. A week later, President Obama gave a funeral eulogy to a congregation in the TD Arena of the College of Charleston, which was packed with more than five thousand people inside, and more outside in the sweltering heat. Even by the standards of that brilliant presidential orator, what happened that day proved a spellbinding experience: unforgettable for those present and stirring even for the calloused journalists who covered the story.

Obama spoke with intellectual and emotional insight—all marked by the profound misery of the occasion.[4] As he spoke, the president returned time and again to the concept of grace, naming each of the murdered victims as he spoke. The word and concept *grace* drifted through the oration, almost like the descant to a hymn. Quoting from President Kennedy ("I look forward to an America which will not be afraid of grace and beauty"), Obama offered a carefully chosen account of the idea of grace and how it reflected the life and work of Reverend Pinckney. He noted that, "according to the Christian tradition, grace is not earned. Grace is not merited. It's not something we deserve. Rather, grace is the free and benevolent favor of God."[5] Obama carefully paced his oration, and as it evolved, the huge gathering—and the clerics assembled behind the president—were moved to respond, adding their own voices to Obama's words. It was as if Obama had become a presiding preacher to his own vast congregation, playing to their feelings, to their biblical knowledge, and to their Christian faith. Eventually, Obama turned, knowingly, to the presiding bishop behind him, paused—and began to sing "Amazing Grace."

No one could claim that Obama is blessed with a good singing voice, but his rendition of "Amazing Grace" that day was one of the most electrifying moments in modern presidential history: a moment of brilliant and calculated audacity. As Obama began to sing, the organist and musicians assembled for the service hastily took up the unexpected task of following the president's vocal pace and rhythm and providing a suitable musical backing. Suddenly and unexpectedly, a presidential eulogy had become a choral moment recognizable to anyone familiar with the musical tradition of African American churches. There were unmistakable echoes of the call-and-response songs from the cotton fields of slave days.[6]

Obama's singing looked and sounded spontaneous. It seemed as though the most powerful man in the land had been swept along on a tide of grief and sadness, succumbing to the emotional power of the occasion. In fact, the president had spent a great deal of time prior to the funeral thinking and talking about singing that hymn. At first he was unsure about whether he should sing. When he raised the question with his wife and advisors, they thought it a bad idea. But Obama explained that if, on the day, he felt that the congregation was on his side, singing "Amazing Grace" would have the desired impact. And how could a largely African American audience not be on the side of the nation's first Black president at such an emotional event? On the day, Obama quickly realized that he had the support of that huge congregation: the moment was indeed right to sing. The impact was exhilarating. In retrospect, it was regarded "as one of the most powerful moments of his Presidency."[7]

I've watched and listened to that event many times, and repetition does not dim the brilliance of the moment—it continues to have a spine-tingling effect. What did it matter that Obama couldn't sing very well? It was a sensational and deeply moving moment that impelled first the assembled clerics around the president, then the whole congregation, to rise and sing along with their president. Equally striking, no one seemed to need a printed copy of the hymn to join in. "Amazing Grace" was as familiar to most people there as the words of the national anthem. A huge assembly of American citizens were, in an instant, revealed to be word perfect with the hymn "Amazing Grace." On that day in June 2015 in Charleston, thousands of Americans, without the printed words to hand, joined their president in singing a familiar hymn. Moreover, they were singing a hymn that is perhaps the most famous piece of writing from the pen of an Atlantic slave trader ... It seems an odd historical twist that brought together that president, that hymn, and that city to create such a memorable occasion.

. . .

The city of Charleston, the College of Charleston, and the hymn "Amazing Grace"—each has its own distinctive link to slavery. The port of Charleston was at the center of slavery in colonial North America and was the place where gunfire heralded the start of the US Civil War. The college was founded in 1770, when that port was the major disembarkation point for enslaved Africans destined for the expanding slave frontiers of colonial North America. Some 40 percent of *all* the Africans shipped to North America landed in Charleston. Across the entire history of the Atlantic trade, more than two hundred thousand Africans landed in the Carolinas and Georgia.[8] Inevitably, the College of Charleston itself was entangled with slavery and with the legacy of the slave past; enslaved labor helped in its early construction, and a number of its trustees, faculty members, and leaders were slave owners. After the Civil War, the college remained defiantly segregationist, and almost went bankrupt in the vain effort to resist integration in the 1960s. National and local pressures finally saw the first African American students enroll in 1967.

The hymn sung by President Obama at the College of Charleston in 2015 was itself born of slavery. It was written in 1772 in the small English town of Olney by the Reverend John Newton, who had, by then, put behind him his former life as the master of a Liverpool slave ship. On one slave ship voyage, in August 1749, Newton had himself landed at Charleston, as first mate on the Liverpool slave ship the *Brownlow,* and had helped to disembark 156 enslaved Africans there.[9] It was a new vessel of a mere fifty tons with a crew of twenty and it had trawled for eight months along the Gold Coast and the Windward Coast, collecting 218 enslaved Africans. By the time it docked at Charleston however, via Antigua, only 156 Africans had survived. The *Brownlow* had suffered a catastrophic loss of life. A slave uprising had cost the lives of four Africans and one crew member; most of the African fatalities had been caused by highly contagious diseases—notably dysentery. In late August, the surviving Africans were advertised for sale "on reasonable terms" at a store on Broad Street.

At first glance, these issues—Charleston, slave ships, "Amazing Grace," and President Obama—might seem to be linked only by the historical imagination. In fact, what unites them, and what fixes them in popular memory, is the complex history of Atlantic slavery.

· · ·

Few hymns have acquired the widespread fame, resonance, or poignancy of "Amazing Grace." It is played today by lone pipers and major orchestras, in moments of personal isolation and on state occasions. "Amazing Grace" has long since slipped its original moorings in Christian worship to become an anthem familiar to millions. It is, at once, a song for our times and a hymn for everyone. But this was not always the case. So how did this happen? How did a simple Christian hymn, designed merely to accompany a sermon delivered by the Reverend John Newton, come to hold such sway over millions in all corners of the modern world? What follows seeks to offer an explanation.

ONE

The Young Sinner

JOHN NEWTON, THE AUTHOR of "Amazing Grace" is, today, best known as a powerful and much-respected cleric whose voice was raised in Britain— to great effect—on behalf of the abolition of the slave trade in the late 1780s. But before he became a hymn-writer, cleric, and abolitionist, Newton's life was dominated by seafaring—and the maritime story of Britain in the eighteenth century was inextricably linked to the Atlantic slave trade.

Newton was born in 1725 in Wapping, a major center of maritime trade on the Thames, with a multitude of industries maintaining and servicing the ships that crowded the riverside— all fresh from trade to and from Europe and the wider world. His father—also John—was a mariner, one of the large number of tough men, drawn from all corners of Britain and around the globe, who made a precarious living from Britain's expanding maritime empire. At the time, London dominated British trade, and the bulk of the nation's imports and exports flowed through the capital. What had first been noticed in Lisbon and Amsterdam two centuries before was now evident in London: goods, commodities, people—and even animals—from the far corners of the world spilled out into local life from the ships arriving from Africa, India, Asia, and the Americas.

John Newton Sr. saw little of his son, but eventually steered him towards a maritime career. Newton Sr. was a well-educated man, though without any firm religious convictions. However his wife, Elizabeth, belonged to the tiny band of Independents, a sect that had emerged in the British Civil War a century earlier and that believed in the autonomy of local congregations. She grounded her son in her own dissenting beliefs, though in later life, Newton made his name in the Church of England. From an early age, the younger John Newton was a keen reader and was soon familiar with biblical learning. His mother also planted a love of hymns in the young John Newton, especially those of Isaac Watts. Though this dissenting influence on John Newton ended with his mother's death when he was only seven, it left its mark: "I could not at once forget the religious impressions I received in my childhood, they often returned to me, but still fainter and fainter." Throughout his early adult years, Newton succumbed to sexual temptations, but at the same time he returned time and again to the "disciplines of prayer, reading Scripture, diary-keeping, and edifying reading."[1] The lessons acquired at his mother's knee never deserted him.

When his father remarried, Newton was sent to a school in Essex. He hated the school, grieved for his mother, and felt excluded from his father's new family. For the rest of his life Newton lamented the breakup of his family life, idealizing his early years with his mother. Yet despite that, he was to be instrumental in the breakup and destruction of the lives of many hundreds of other people. As a sailor and then as captain of a slave ship, he helped to transport huge numbers of Africans across the Atlantic, all of whom had been torn away from their families and communities. Here was yet another aspect of the life of John Newton and his contemporaries which many, today, find perplexing.

.   .   .

Newton's life at sea began at the age of eleven in 1736 when he joined his father on a voyage to the Mediterranean. It was the first of many maritime ventures and heralded a period of youthful indulgence that alternated with periods of deep religiosity. "I learned to curse and blaspheme, and was extremely wicked. . . . All this before I was twelve years old." Later, in his teens, he confessed that "I loved sin, and was unwilling to forsake it."[2] Throughout, Newton remained an avid reader and always had a book to hand while at sea. When, aged seventeen, he read *Characteristicks,* a book of essays by Lord Shaftesbury, he experienced a profound change in his attitude to religion: Shaftesbury's essays released him from any attachment to established faith. He became his own man, able to set aside religious orthodoxy and to make up his own mind about theological issues. Henceforth he no longer hesitated to proclaim his views. Newton's struggles with theology took place as he continued to lead an occasionally profligate life, vacillating between the excess of his fellow seafarers and his inner attachment to the faith first nurtured by his late mother.

For all his book-learning and regular reading, Newton was an undisciplined young man, never at ease with authority, bouncing from one post to another and failing to settle down to whatever work his father found for him. His father, anxious to see his son settled, persuaded a friend, the Liverpool merchant and slave trader Joseph Manesty, to offer his son a position in Jamaica, where Britain's slave economy was booming. All this was thrown into confusion when, on visiting family friends in Chatham, Newton fell hopelessly in love with their fourteen-year-old daughter, Mary Catlett: "Almost at the first sight of this girl . . . I was impressed with an affection for her, which never abated or lost its influence a single moment in my heart from that hour."[3] Newton missed his ship and missed the chance to work in Jamaica, but Manesty gave him another chance, this time on one of his merchant ships trading in the Mediterranean.

What followed was a remarkable confusion of events in Newton's life, a jumble of indiscipline and thoughtlessness that might easily have brought his life to a premature end. Press-ganged into the Royal Navy, assailed by the coarseness and crude disbelief of fellow sailors, and pining for his lost love, Newton broke one naval rule after another. Most serious of all he deserted his ship—HMS *Harwich*—now en route to Gambia. His despairing captain was glad to be rid of him, transferring him to a merchant vessel in Madeira. Despite all this, Newton continued to defy authority, and he was again transferred. This time however he went into the dangerous world of trading in slaves on the coast of West Africa. It was a period when, in his own words "my whole life, when awake, was a course of the most horrid impiety and profaneness. I know not that I have ever since met so daring a blasphemer."[4] Threatened with a return to a British warship, Newton opted to work for a European slave trader, based on Plantain Island off the coast of Sierra Leone. It proved to be the low point of his life. He was sick, despised by his employer's wife, who starved and maltreated him, and reduced to what he regarded as little better than wretched slavery. The experience did little, however, to moderate his own behavior towards enslaved Africans in later years. He felt lucky to escape his misery when offered work by another European and he moved to other work involved with slaving on the African coast.

Throughout this troubled period, John Newton's father had no idea what had happened to his son. Keen to find out, he alerted the captain of the *Greyhound,* one of Manesty's ships trading on the African coast, to be on the lookout for his missing son. By a series of lucky breaks, the *Greyhound* discovered him, and Newton was persuaded to join that vessel on its prolonged trading voyage, for a range of African goods, along the African coast. Finally, in January 1748, the vessel sailed west into the Atlantic, thence to sail back to Liverpool.

Sailing from West Africa to Liverpool involved a voyage of seven thousand miles, because the vessel had first to sail towards Brazil "on account of the trade winds," then north to Newfoundland where they stocked up with cod from the teeming local banks. The *Greyhound* left Newfoundland waters on March 1, in a hard westerly gale that pushed the ship across the Atlantic. After such a protracted and grueling time at sea, mainly on the coast of West Africa, the ship was in poor condition and in no state to cope with the severe Atlantic storm that soon engulfed them. Battered by mountainous seas, the rigging and part of the superstructure swept away, the *Greyhound* was reduced to a floating wreck. The crew baled and pumped out the water: some roped themselves to the ship to avoid being washed overboard. After days of struggle, the storm abated and Newton, who had turned to his Bible, musing on his fate and on the Lord's ability to save, "thought I saw the hand of God displayed in our favour." Thereafter, every year, Newton marked March 21 as the day he was saved and he gave himself over to a day of reflection. As the *Greyhound* closed on Ireland, the storms returned and by the time they landed in Ireland on April 8 the ship was barely afloat, its crew utterly exhausted, their provisions consumed or destroyed.[5]

Newton had passed through a tempestuous seaborne experience that transformed his life and his outlook. Though he recognized his continuing deep personal flaws and weaknesses, his narrow escape from drowning utterly transformed him: "I was a new man."[6] The foundations had been laid for Newton's rejection of his old habits. Newton's narrow escape from death was a turning point. He believed himself to have been saved by God's intervention: by God's grace. Years later he wrote to a friend, "Surely no one could be a greater libertine in principle or practice, more abandoned or more daring than I. But I obtained mercy. I hardly feel any stronger proof of remaining depravity than in my having so faint a sense of the Amazing Grace that snatched me from ruin, that pardoned such enormous sins, preserved my life when I stood upon the brink of eternity and could only be preserved by miracle."[7]

. . .

Throughout his teenage years at sea, John Newton had been an avid reader, buying books wherever he landed and struggling with the religious principles imparted by his devout mother. Elizabeth Newton had instilled in her son a highly disciplined love of reading—and worship. She read Bible stories to him, teaching him to respond to the catechisms and to memorize hymns and psalms, especially those written for children. Elizabeth loved the hymns of Isaac Watts and her son inevitably followed. They were hymns noted for their simplicity, using ordinary, comprehensible language and were quite unlike the impenetrable Latin-based worship of the Church of England at that time. Watts's hymns were an aspect of the ongoing Reformation that wrenched worship free from an exclusive, Latin-based priesthood and relocated it among ordinary people, simply by using the common vernacular. While worshiping at the chapel of Dr. David Jennings in Wapping in 1755, Newton's head was filled with "many valuable pieces, chapters, and portions of scriptures, catechisms, hymns and poems."[8]

Newton's mother had left him with a love for the printed word. Newton was a classic example of the autodidact, finding enlightenment in the world of print and spending hours poring over his Bible. Wherever the young Newton docked, he headed for the nearest bookshop. His purchase, aged seventeen, of the popular collection of essays by the Earl of Shaftesbury, *Characteristicks,* proved to be a revelation to the young Newton. He read it time and again and it released Newton from adherence to the established Church. Henceforth, he was determined to set aside accepted religious orthodoxy and seek his own path towards Christian truth—and all this by the age of seventeen.

Newton's newfound confidence in theological matters did not, however, change his social and personal life. In the shipboard presence of his father, he was, of necessity, a disciplined youth. By nature, however, he was volatile and undisciplined. In later life he looked back with shame on his youthful indiscretions: "I was capable of anything. I had not the least fear of God before my eyes, nor (so far as I can remember) the least sensibility of conscience."[9]

In the years when John Newton lived and worked on ships involved in the African trade, and when he worked as a slaver in West Africa, he had entered a world where, by his own account, "I now might be as abandoned as I pleased without any control."[10] For all his prior and subsequent avowals of piety, the young John Newton had plunged into the vicious, violent, and sexually predatory world of Atlantic slavery and slave ships.

As an older man, Newton clearly regretted the excesses of his younger days, both at sea and in Africa. At the time, however, his behavior was commonplace among the men involved in the enslavement and transportation of Africans. Though the power and prospects of the sailors and the enslaved Africans were starkly different, the slave ship was a violent world of fear for both Africans and sailors, and everywhere there lurked the dangers of disease and sudden death. Life on a slave ship was hellish, yet every maritime nation, on both sides of the Atlantic, dispatched ship after ship into the maws of the slaving system: whatever the human risks, it was a trade that promised profit and bounty to successful white survivors. John Newton was to be among the lucky ones in that he survived the slave ships and prospered from them.

In his later writings, Newton recalled how he had emerged from the wretchedness of the misery he had endured in Africa to personal triumph: he had been saved from the pit of despair. Yet in these first years after the *Greyhound* experience, Newton failed to realize (or to acknowledge publicly) that his redemption coexisted with his continuing trade in and brutalizing of enslaved Africans. At first, he saw no conflict between his own salvation and his role in condemning Africans to slavery.

. . .

The man who had provided John Newton with so many opportunities, the Liverpool merchant Joseph Manesty, personified the aggressive and ambitious outlook of that city's merchants in the mid-eighteenth century. He was the major partner in at least nine ships and part owner of several others. As he admitted to an American merchant, "no trade [was] push'd with so much sprit as the African." Indeed, it was Liverpool's trade to Africa that enabled that port to overtake both London and Bristol in mercantile importance. As Liverpool boomed, there was a resulting shortage both of ships and sailors. Manesty wrote that "ships are so scarce here that none is to be had at any rate." As a result, he commissioned shipbuilders in Rhode Island to construct a slavery vessel for him, laying down specific details of what was required, from the kind of timbers to be used to the most minute measurements of the vessel. The ship's sides were to be flared "for the more commodious stowing [of] Negroes twixt Decks." With a keen eye on costs, Manesty shipped to Rhode Island those items of equipment (sails, anchors, metalware) that were cheaper in Liverpool, to be added to the American-built ship.[11] Less easily acquired were reliable, experienced men to command such vessels.

INSURRECTION ON BOARD A SLAVE SHIP.

FIGURE 1. Like all slave ship captains, John Newton faced African resistance crossing the Atlantic. W. L. Walton, "Insurrection on Board a Slave Ship," in William Fox, *Brief History of Wesleyan Missions on the Western Coast of Africa* (London: Aylott and Jones, 1851). Lithograph. Library Company of Philadelphia, 12623.O.

The ideal captain of a slave ship had to possess a variety of qualities: he had to be a competent mariner, stern (sometimes fierce) commander of invariably difficult crewmen, a sharp-eyed trader on the African coast, and head jailer of a ship crowded with desperate African prisoners. Though the rewards for the master of a successful voyage could be high, the risks and dangers were immense. So severe was the shortage of ships' masters that shipowners often had few options about their choice of captain. Thus it was, in 1748, that Joseph Manesty offered John Newton the command of one of his slave ships, the *Brownlow*. By then, Newton was an experienced seafarer, mainly in the Mediterranean, and though he had spent a long period working a slaver on the West African coast, he had never commanded a ship.

Doubtless aware of the dangers, Newton wisely declined the offer, opting instead to travel as first mate on the *Brownlow*'s next slaving voyage, where it was to purchase newly enslaved Africans and transport them to South Carolina for sale. Departing Liverpool in July 1748, the voyage was to be a harsh baptism in the brutal realities of slave trading. Newton spent his time on the African coast negotiating for slaves on shore and ferrying the captives back to the mother ship. It was exhausting and dangerous work: African resistance and the threat of Atlantic rollers both posed permanent dangers. More dangerous still were tropical diseases, which swept away a number of Newton's crew. The vessel departed from the Gold Coast with 218 enslaved men, women, and children packed below decks. As was frequent, in mid-Atlantic the enslaved Africans rose up against their captors in a desperate bid for freedom; the crew suppressed the uprising with widespread killing. By the time the *Brownlow* reached Charleston, the vessel had lost sixty-two Africans to disease and in the crew's suppression of African resistance—a death rate of more than 28 percent, high even by the brutal standards of slave ships.[12]

· · ·

On that voyage, Newton experienced the full range of slave-trading dangers: the dangers of the work of purchasing slaves on the West African coast, the enormous toll of death from disease and violent suppression of insurrection, and all the risks involved in Atlantic sailing itself, before arriving at Charleston (Charles Town as it was known at the time) via Antigua in August 1749. Though his ship had inflicted terrible loss of life on its African captives, the survivors were eagerly purchased by local slave owners. In late August, the *South Carolina Gazette* advertised "a choice parcel of healthy slaves, just arrived from the Windward Coast of Africa in the snow *Brownlow*." They were available "on reasonable terms" at a store run by Kennan and Campbell on Broad Street. The storeowners also offered "a parcel of choice Madeira wine to sell."[13]

Today, Charleston's Broad Street presents itself as an attractive urban mix of civic, religious, and commercial buildings, an image used to promote tourism to the city. Even when Newton explored the city, it was thought to be a "neat pretty place." A resident, writing in 1765, noted that "it contains about 1,000 houses, with inhabitants, 5,000 whites and 20,000 blacks." The wider region—what was to become South Carolina—had a semitropical climate, rich in a variety of resources, notably timber and naval stores, and offered great potential for the cultivation of valuable export crops. For that, white property owners needed enslaved Africans: "The laborious business is here chiefly done by black slaves of which there are great multitudes."[14] The men, women, and children who were the *Brownlow*'s cargo were sold in six weeks, and then scattered—who knows where—to a variety of settlers and planters around the city and its hinterland. They were also assigned new names— or numbers—by people who entered them on their paperwork as items of trade. They entered America as chattel.

For his part, John Newton showed no interest in the enslaved or their fate. Once relieved of his shipboard duties, he was content to enjoy the social life of Charleston. His time in the town was a period of continuing vagueness, unsure of where his spiritual journey should take him, and he spent much of his spare time there listening to local preachers and taking walks in neighboring woods "in the exercise of prayer and praise." Yet he spent his evenings "in vain and worthless company" though "my strongest desires were towards the things of God."[15] To the modern reader, Newton presents a puzzling image. Here was a man who seemed increasingly concerned with spiritual matters, who read voraciously in the Scriptures and in classical texts, and who sought out and listened to clerics from a variety of different denominations. Yet he lived with the stench of the slave ships in his nostrils. In retrospect, he was just one of the more famous of men who saw no inconsistency, no conflict, between their religious convictions and their complicity with African slavery.

. . .

By the time Newton returned to Liverpool in December 1749, he was all too familiar with the dangers of the Atlantic slave trade. Yet its rewards seemed to outweigh the risks, especially for a young man keen to show his prospective father-in-law that he had the wherewithal to care for his intended bride, Mary Catlett.

His employer, Joseph Manesty, was clearly impressed by Newton's work as first mate on the *Brownlow,* and again offered him the command of one of his slave ships. It came with the tempting prospects of the financial rewards of a successful slave-trading voyage. With such promised bounty to hand, Newton hurried to the Catlett home in Chatham intent on proposing to Mary. Though she twice refused his marriage proposal, his third attempt succeeded. He and Mary married on February 12, 1750. It proved a happy marriage that lasted until Mary's death in 1790, and John Newton continued to adore her for the rest of his life—even publishing his letters to her in 1793. Three months after their wedding, Newton returned to Liverpool as captain of Manesty's slave ship, the *Duke of Argyle.*

The ship, a poor old vessel, hardly fit "to make a Gravesend voyage" in the words of its master, left Liverpool in August 1750 bound for the Windward Coast (modern Liberia and the Ivory Coast), then to Antigua, with a crew of thirty; Newton planned to fill the holds with 250 newly enslaved African men, women, and children. That such a wretched vessel was used to carry hundreds of enslaved people is revealing of Liverpool's booming slave business: these were thriving years for Liverpool merchants, who used any ship they could lay their hands on. The crew was as wretched as the ship; they were, in Newton's words, "the refuse and dregs of the Nation."[16] During the first seven months of the trip, when the ship was on the coast purchasing slaves, Newton had trouble with the crew—drunkenness, violence, absenteeism—and no amount of punishment seemed to work. Newton was obliged to exchange the worst offenders for men from a Royal Naval ship, handing over his troublemakers to the tender mercies of the severe discipline in the Royal Navy.

Negotiating with African traders and dignitaries on the Windward Coast, in what Newton described as a "warlike peace," Newton slowly filled the *Argyle* with enslaved men, women, and children. There followed the usual weeks of dangers as growing numbers of desperate people were packed into the increasingly crowded, squalid conditions of the slave decks. There was little he could do about violent death and disease, which raced through both crew and captives. The crew suppressed a well-organized revolt, and Newton thought they had survived by "Favour of Providence" and hoped that "Divine assistance" would see them through such dangers until they landed in Antigua in July 1751.[17]

John Newton's first voyage as master was not as successful as Joseph Manesty had hoped: the *Argyle* lost 28 of the 164 captive Africans and 7 of the 30 crewmen. Throughout the voyage, John Newton had continued his personal, intellectual engagement with theology, reading the Scriptures, musing about the mysteries of God's doings, and seeking ways of finding grace. To modern eyes Newton was an astonishing example of what Dickens was later to describe as "telescopic philanthropy," not noticing matters close to hand while looking at distant issues: "I never knew sweeter or more frequent hours of divine communion than in my two last voyages to Guinea."[18] As he strolled the deck, Newton marveled at God's great creation—the ocean and the heavens—but seemed not to notice the stinking miseries endured by hundreds of newly enslaved men, women, and children shackled only a few feet below his quarters. When he landed in St. Kitts, he fretted about an anticipated letter from his wife, Mary, which had gone to Antigua. He persuaded himself that she had died. He was so worried he could not eat and felt unwell. Yet he had, in the same period, casually consigned dead enslaved people to the deep, their bodies simply tossed over the side on the slow haul across the Atlantic. In the brutal economy of enslavement, the dead were disposed of with little notice by their captors, except for the loss of profit entailed. The numbers assigned to the enslaved when they came on board were simply scratched from Newton's log of the voyage.

Here was a white man of enormous passion and love for his distant wife but who (like almost everyone involved in slave trading) showed no compassion or sympathy for his own Black victims.

· · ·

Newton's first voyage as slave captain clearly satisfied Joseph Manesty who, in June 1752, gave him command of the *African*—a much better, newer ship, custom-built for slaving. The vessel may have been better, but the familiar difficulties with crewmen persisted: drunkenness, thieving, and all-round indiscipline. Newton dared not take his eye off them. The enslaved Africans posed, to his eyes, their own threat of attempted escape and violent resistance. Yet throughout all this turbulence and danger, Newton wrote regular loving letters to his wife, Mary, and continued to reflect about his spiritual struggles. Here was a man who doled out the most severe of punishments to his crew and savage violence to the Africans he held captive, before sitting down in the captain's cabin to write gentle love letters to his distant wife, then drafting intellectual musings about theology. By late June 1753, he had delivered and sold 167 Africans to St. Kitts. This had clearly been a profitable venture, and the pious Newton was able to send his wife the considerable sums of £50 and £207.[19]

Throughout that voyage, Newton imposed a strict personal regime on himself: time devoted to self-improvement and always time set aside for worship and "to keep a sense of dependence upon God's bounty and the free Grace of the Saviour." He kept the Sabbath holy, rising early, pacing the deck, praying, reading the Scriptures—and writing. He also tried to engage his crew in worship. As he crossed the Atlantic after selling his second cargo of enslaved people, Newton was frequently struck by his good fortune, and the long weeks sailing back to Liverpool gave him plenty of time for prolonged biblical study and thought. There were moments when he burst into tears thinking about his good fortune "and was from thence brought upon my knees (as I trust) by the impression of the Holy Spirit, to humble myself for my unworthiness."[20]

While John Newton enjoyed his time in St. Kitts in the summer of 1753, the Africans he had delivered began a lifetime's bondage in the deadly sugar plantations. Newton, however, was handsomely entertained by local planters and merchants, his fine singing voice put to good use at their evening social gatherings. At one such enjoyable assembly, Newton encountered another ship's captain who was to play an important role in

Newton's religious life. Alexander Clunie was master of ship from Wapping and, when at home, was a member of an Independent church in Stepney. Like Newton, Clunie was steeped in biblical learning and devotion. Over a period of four weeks the two men met on each other's ships, discussing their mutual interests and exploring the complexities of their faith. For all his reading, Newton was afraid of temptation and worried about slipping back to his old wicked ways. Clunie convinced him that he would be saved, "not by my own power and holiness" but by "the mighty power and promise of God." Newton henceforth believed that through the Lord's grace, as opposed to deeds, he was ensured of a heavenly fate.[21] The Lord's amazing grace ensured the salvation of the wretch that John Newton felt himself to be. It was also an important meeting for Clunie, for he resolved thereafter to keep a diary, and urged Newton to do the same. That encounter in St. Kitts laid the basis for two of the most important documents we possess about the Atlantic slave trade and the devotional lives of participants in that trade: the diaries kept by John Newton and Alexander Clunie.[22]

That the captains of two ships docked at St. Kitts—in the midst of the filth, violence, and horror of slavery—should spend countless evenings locked in deep discussion about theology might baffle many modern readers. No less curious perhaps, their congenial discussions laid the foundations for the hymn that was to become a popular anthem three centuries later.

Newton left St. Kitts on the seven-week voyage back to Liverpool, buoyed by the inspiration of Clunie's words. He also carried with him the names of suitable contacts provided by Clunie: people in London who would be happy to further Newton's religious learning and education. More important perhaps, Clunie had given Newton the confidence to be more open about his faith: to pray aloud, to speak up for God in whatever company he found himself. Newton now accepted that his past sins and transgressions were behind him, and that he was saved by the Lord's grace. Newton came to believe that his own life was a living example of the Lord's grace. Henceforth the concept of grace—and the very word itself—was embedded in John Newton's mind. It was a word which recurred time and again in the prodigious volumes of writings that tumbled from this hugely industrious man.

The *African* docked in Liverpool on August 7, 1754, and Newton returned home effectively a new man, resolved to preach, to spread the gospel, and to persuade others, whatever their transgressions, that they too could secure the Lord's grace: they need not strive for grace by themselves, because it was a gift from the Almighty. In the brutal squalor of an Atlantic slave ship, the seed of "Amazing Grace" had been sown.

TWO

Slave Trader Turned Preacher

CAPTAIN JOHN NEWTON HAD NOT LOST a single crewman on his last voyage, on the *African,* and he promptly gave thanks in various churches in Liverpool. But as he was preparing for his next voyage, in a new Manesty vessel, the *Bee,* Newton was suddenly struck down by what he described as "a fit." It was a stroke and it instantly eliminated him from further work at sea. His wife, Mary, was thrown into depression by his illness, though she recovered quickly. A return to the slave trade was now out of the question, but Joseph Manesty once again came to Newton's rescue, securing for him the post of surveyor of Liverpool's tides and as supervisor of inbound and outbound vessels. Newton spent his free time attending a great variety of local churches, reading their literature and, following Clunie's advice, discussing theology with anyone willing to talk with him. Like many others at the time, on both sides of the Atlantic, Newton was especially impressed by George Whitefield, a key inspiration behind the rise of Methodism and whose preaching held an astonishing sway over congregations. Above all, Newton liked the way Whitefield used hymns and hymn-singing in his services.

Newton's search for spiritual peace took place in a period of remarkable evangelical revival, when people were urged to follow the Lord by resolving to change their lives and to cast aside their former ways. Few were more conscious of their sinful pasts, and of the need to change their ways, than the slave trader John Newton. Reflecting on his life as a slave trader, Newton wrote, "I only thought myself bound to treat the slaves under my care with gentleness, and to consult their ease and convenience." Again, the modern reader is likely to find Newton's self-defense both mealy-mouthed and unconvincing. He wrote of his "prayers that the Lord in His own time, would be pleased to fix me in a more humane calling."[1] After 1754, his time had come. Newton's lifetime attachment to self-education and industrious study now had a focus: he was determined to become a preacher.

As he picked his way through Liverpool's different congregations, he scrutinized other preachers' failings and their strengths. In the process his own interventions and remarks in churches began to be noticed.[2] Even John Wesley was impressed.[3] But, for all his ambition and learning, Newton was self-taught, with no form of qualification, and entry to the Church required either a university degree or an influential patron. For seven years, Newton tried unsuccessfully to become a cleric in the Church of England, only to be rebuffed time and again. He was refused ordination twice by the archbishop of York, twice by the bishop of Chester, and once by the archbishop of Canterbury. A man of lesser resolve would surely have given up the quest.[4] Yet Newton was a man of considerable intellect and resilience.

Fortunately for his ambitions, his erudite letters (which he produced in great numbers, scattering them to learned and sympathetic correspondents) caught the attention of influential friends, notably Lord Dartmouth, one of the country's most prominent evangelicals. Dartmouth was hugely impressed by Newton's letters and sponsored their publication. In a rather meandering fashion, Newton's letters formed an autobiography, which was both an account of his life and a diary of his soul. They also provided revealing information about Newton's life as a slave trader, though sometimes the letters were more revealing for what Newton overlooked rather than for what he said.

Lord Dartmouth was a major landowner and as such had the patronage of a number of parishes. After meeting Newton, and being convinced of his suitability for the church, Dartmouth arranged for Newton to be appointed curate of the parish of Olney, a small town in Buckinghamshire. After overcoming a string of last-minute bureaucratic problems, John

FIGURE 2. St. Peter and St. Paul Church, Olney, England, where John Newton was curate from 1764 to 1780 and where "Amazing Grace" was first sung on January 1, 1773. Photograph by Brian Tomlinson, 2021. CC BY 2.0.

Newton was admitted to holy orders by the bishop of Lincoln on April 29, 1764, a decade after he stepped ashore in Liverpool from his last voyage as a slave captain. He had struggled for a decade to stake his claim as a cleric. Now, all those years after ill-health had forced him to abandon slave trading, he had entered a new calling.

Newton was now poised to make his mark, able to speak not only to his two thousand local parishioners, but also, through his preaching, writings—and eventually his hymns—to the world at large. Newton set about his parochial work with relish, and his powerful preaching soon filled the church, which had to be extended to cope with the growing numbers. He established what was effectively a Sunday school for local children, and quickly endeared himself to local people via his pastoral activities among the poor and the sick. No sooner had Newton settled in Olney than he acquired national fame, thanks to Lord Dartmouth's sponsorship of the publication of his letters. His old seafaring friend

Alexander Clunie from the St. Kitts encounter had a hand in printing the book. Money from sales of the book proved vital to the ill-paid curate and his wife. The book also inspired another benefactor to provide Newton with an annual gift of two hundred pounds to support his work in Olney.

Though the foundations for Newton's life as a preacher had been laid long before he arrived at Olney, it was there, among local agricultural workers and lacemakers, that he honed his considerable skills as an orator and as a clerical writer and publicist. Newton had commanded the roughest of men at sea and had no trouble speaking to local working people who had no formal learning, preaching in a manner and a language they recognized and respected. Along with many others, Newton was acutely aware that the Church of England's sermons were infamously dull, often numbingly boring, and sometimes impenetrably scholarly: they were often an invitation to snooze rather than to listen and think. So, from the start, Newton set out to be different and to catch the locals' attention, sprinkling his sermons with tales from his seafaring life—often on the spur of the moment, whenever a thought came to mind. It was as if the preaching at Olney had shifted gears: Newton switched attention from the educated classes to the common folk, and they, in turn, responded by turning up in growing numbers. He caught the public's attention, much as his hymns were to do later. People walked many miles to listen to the new man in the pulpit. Even after the church had been extended to cater for the expanding congregations, overspill meetings had to be held in the nearby empty great house belonging to Lord Dartmouth.[5]

But John Newton was not satisfied simply to be a successful preacher. He enjoyed singing—in church and in social gatherings—and he wanted people to join him.

. . .

Newton had long been impressed by the importance of hymn-singing in church and regularly noted its impact. At Chatham in 1755, he remarked

FIGURE 3. The Reverend John Newton, 1725–1807. Line engraving by Joseph Collyer the Younger, after oil painting by John Russell, "Rev'd John Newton, late Rector of the United Parishes of St. Mary Woolnoth and St. Mary Woolchurch Haw. Born at London 24th July 1725. O.S. Died 21st of Dec-r 1807," 1808. By permission of Trustees of Cowper and Newton Museum, Olney, Buckinghamshire.

how local worshippers spent their time "in singing & repeating hymns of praise." Later, in Liverpool, he noted how a local congregation "concluded with a hymn."[6] Once settled in Olney, it was inevitable that Newton would employ hymns as an important feature of his ministry. He had begun to write hymns in Liverpool in 1763, but it was at Olney that Newton's hymn-writing flourished. On Sunday evenings, small gatherings in his home "spend an hour or more in prayer and singing."[7] He distributed hymnbooks to the children at his evening classes and employed a Mr. Hull to teach local children to sing.

In 1767 John Newton made friends with the much-troubled poet William Cowper, then thirty-six, who had already passed through bouts of deep and recurring depression and a number of suicide attempts. Through family and friendly contacts, Cowper moved to Olney and the two men struck up an immediate friendship. Newton invited Cowper to join him in working on a volume of hymns he was compiling. The eventual outcome was the *Olney Hymns,* published in 1779.

The arrival of William Cowper inaugurated the most creative period of Newton's own hymn-writing, and throughout the 1770s Newton regularly wrote hymns for the prayer meetings held after tea, which took place in Lord Dartmouth's empty but spacious great house in Olney. Sometimes, Newton offered a discourse on the hymn's theme. It was soon clear that the two men, the troubled poet and the charismatic preacher, were destined to publish hymns as a joint venture, though the project was cast into doubt by Cowper's recurring mental illness. Newton pressed on, writing a huge number of hymns, some for specific local occasions—a death in the community, for example. Throughout, Newton was aware that he was writing, as indeed he was preaching, to a much wider audience than the good folks of Olney. Long before the publication of the *Olney Hymns* in 1779, some of his hymns had been published in a number of religious outlets, normally as a result of Newton having included the hymns in a letter to a sympathetic friend or supporter. But even in his most optimistic moments, Newton could never have imagined that his words would, in time, reach (and move) tens of millions of people.

. . .

Newton became an active hymn-writer at a time when hymns were relatively new in England. The English hymn "came of age" in 1707, with Isaac Watts's *Hymns and Spiritual Songs*. Watts's intention was to free worship from the "metrical psalmody" of traditional worship and instead locate the hymn—and the singing of hymns—in a world the congregation would recognize. Henceforth, hymns were to address the here and now. Following Watts, hymnbooks came spinning off the presses throughout the eighteenth century, led by Methodists and Moravians.

When John Wesley traveled to Georgia in 1735, he learned from his Moravian traveling companions "the value of hymn-singing as a corporate expression of faith." Wesley's first hymnbook was published in 1737 when he was in Georgia, and hymn-singing quickly took root among his followers. In fact, Methodism "was born in song."[8] Of course singing in the Christian church was an ancient tradition, introduced as early as the fourth century by St. Ambrose, the archbishop of Milan.[9] But most church singing was done by the clergy. That changed with the Reformation when congregations began to sing the psalms. Singing psalms was especially important for the Puritans, and Puritan settlers transplanted the practice into North America in the seventeenth century. The spread of printed material in that same century saw a proliferation of books of hymns and psalms.[10]

The Church of England—sluggish and unwilling to change on all fronts—resisted the trend towards hymn-singing effectively until the early nineteenth century, but by then, dissenting voices had produced huge numbers of hymnbooks and many memorable hymns. As a result, the choral culture of English worship changed beyond all recognition. Congregations across the country were singing as never before, and many of the hymns they loved became classic and popular choral pieces which survive to this day, having traveled all round the globe. In the words of John Newton, "Some of us here, know that the Lord has comforted us by Hymns, which express Scriptural truths."[11]

When Newton began to write hymns in Olney, the choral tradition had moved beyond Isaac Watts. It had adopted more popular musical forms and was now characterized by outbursts of enthusiasm: exclamations—sighs, moans, and groans. A powerful strain of choral elation had entered hymn-singing. It was a trend that inevitably caused controversy, but John Newton pressed on, in his usual indefatigable and self-assured fashion, to bring comfort and biblical understanding to congregations via their own renditions of his hymns. Moreover what emerged from the pens of Newton and Cowper seemed restrained compared to other hymn-singing.[12]

Newton was clearly in the tradition of Isaac Watts, in aiming for a popular audience: he wrote hymns "for the weak and the poor of his flock."[13] Most of Newton's congregations of common folk were however illiterate, and hymnbooks were of little use to them. Yet despite their illiteracy they soon learned the words of the most popular hymns. They did this by the practice of "lining out," in which hymns were spelled out, sung by a minister or choral leader, two lines at a time. Words and lines which had a memorable rhythm or meaning were quickly remembered, and the minister would move onto the next two lines. By repetition and regular practice, a congregation soon learned a full verse and soon a complete hymn—though often prompted by a minister or choir master.

Lining out became a widespread habit among illiterate congregations in the seventeenth century, and it naturally traveled across the Atlantic with migrants to North America. A similar pattern evolved among enslaved Africans, most notably in work songs. Call-and-response songs, with roots in African and European worship, could be heard on slave plantations throughout colonial America.

The cultural habit of lining out survived even after the emergence of widespread popular literacy, especially in isolated communities, and it remained a powerful force in a number of American churches. It was also useful if a large crowd did not have printed verses available. Some hymns seemed ideally suited to lining out: those with short lines, a simple rhythm, and a powerful meaning. A perfect illustration of this was Newton's hymn "Amazing Grace," written in 1772 but first published in the *Olney Hymns* in 1779. It was ideally suited to lining out: the lines were short, the rhythm simple, and the words had an instant, personal appeal. From its first congregations in the eighteenth century, down to President Obama in the twenty-first, "Amazing Grace" was ideally suited to this method of choral singing.

> Amazing Grace! how sweet the sound.
> That sav'd a wretch like me!

.   .   .

Newton did not regard himself as a master hymn-writer: more "a journeyman in the trade ... a skilled versifier, not a sophisticated poet."[14] Despite Newton's claim to be merely a humble versifier, many of his hymns, and especially those written in conjunction with Cowper, contradict his modesty. Both Newton and Cowper were deeply learned in scriptural and poetic literature, and both used that learning when drafting their hymns. They wrote hymns that were aimed at a wide, popular audience, while hoping not to offend worshippers who preferred more elevated, intellectual, and "learned" hymns.

The concept of "grace" was revealed even in the way Newton organized the *Olney Hymns*. They were arranged into three distinct sections, categories shaped by Newton's view of the development of grace. The first group of hymns considered how the sinner was initially alerted to contrition and spiritual desire. The second discussed the question of the testing of the sinner and of divine assistance. The third concerned "a more perfect obedience and resignation to God."[15] "Amazing Grace" was located in the first group.

.   .   .

Newton was a highly disciplined writer and tried to write a hymn each week, hoping to use it alongside his weekly sermon, which was itself linked to a scriptural extract. It is possible to trace each of his hymns to its scriptural inspiration. Many were sung initially in Lord Dartmouth's large house in the village of Olney, where, Newton told a friend, the assembly "is thronged exceedingly."[16] He drafted "Amazing Grace" in December 1772 and it was first sung on New Year's Day, 1773. Analysis has shown how closely the hymn was related to his sermon on that day, and to its associated biblical link, 1 Chronicles 17.[17] The composition also coincided with the grim news that William Cowper had once again slipped into a severe bout of mental illness. Newton tended his friend for hours on end, month after month: a dark period when Cowper was utterly incapacitated, incapable of writing or even of holding a sensible conversation. Between 1767 and 1773 Cowper had spent part of most days with Newton, but now he was completely disabled by mental illness and unshakably convinced that he was damned. No amount of loving care by Newton and doctors could dissuade him from believing that he was doomed. It weighed heavily on Newton himself and for months he found himself unable to write the hymns that had become so important in his local ministry. That year, 1773, saw the end of Cowper's participation in church services.

In the course of the 1770s, a number of Newton's hymns had been published in various religious publications and he had been urged to gather all his hymns into a single volume. When, in 1779, Newton eventually compiled his hymns, together with those he had written with Cowper, he paid generous homage to his friend. In the preface, Newton acknowledged that the Olney hymns formed "a monument, to perpetuate the remembrance of an intimate and endeared friendship."[18] He attached the letter C to each hymn written by Cowper in the collection that followed. Of a total of 348 hymns, Cowper had written 68, Newton 280.[19] The *Olney Hymns* confirmed Newton's reputation as a prodigious hymn-writer. Its publication also marked the end of Newton's time at Olney.

By 1779 Newton was well known far beyond the parish of Olney. After fifteen years there, he moved to the parish of St. Mary Woolnoth in the City of London. His ministry remained much as it had been in a poor rural parish. His days were filled with meetings, parochial duties, endless hours of prayer and worship, and prodigious amounts of letter-writing. Now, however, he was close to the seat of political power, and he moved easily among prominent and influential people in London.

The slave trade that Newton had left twenty years before continued to thrive, with ever more enslaved Africans shipped across the Atlantic in British vessels. The commercial importance of slaving was undiminished—but Britain itself had begun to change. Britain's defeat in the American war in 1783 and loss of the American colonies set in train a number of critical political and social changes. The arrival in England and Canada of large numbers of freed slaves who had sided with the defeated British focused attention on the condition of what became known as London's "black poor." Subsequent efforts to resettle them from London and Nova Scotia to Sierra Leone proved disastrous.[20] But the episode drew attention to the wider issue of slavery, ultimately rallying William Wilberforce as parliamentary leader of the abolition cause—and bringing an African, Olaudah Equiano, to the forefront of political attention, aided by his publication of his remarkable autobiographical *Narrative* in 1789.

It would have been impossible for Newton not to notice the swirl of activity about the slave trade, living as he did so close to the center of political power. Newton had never tried to hide his early years as a slaver, though he was hesitant to spell out some of the more horrific details involved. Moreover, Newton had known Wilberforce since William's childhood. Once persuaded of the need to press for the abolition of the slave trade, Wilberforce naturally called on Newton for help, and for firsthand knowledge about the trade. The former slave trader now found himself at the center of national political debate.

Initiated by Quakers, the British campaign against the slave trade, led by the Society for Effecting the Abolition of the Slave Trade, gathered speed after 1787: Parliament was stirred by Wilberforce, and wide and increasingly popular abolitionist sentiment was directed at Parliament. In trying to marshal a campaign against the slave trade, whose voice could speak more forcibly and persuasively than that of a former slave ship captain? Moreover Newton's was now a celebrated voice, famous as an evangelical preacher and a writer of popular hymns. John Newton was also an obvious choice as a star witness for a committee of the Privy Council convened to gather evidence about the slave trade in 1788. Aged and infirm, Newton was led into the chamber by no less figure than the prime minister, William Pitt. As he entered, in an extraordinary acknowledgment of Newton's eminence, the Privy Council rose to greet him. It was a remarkable political moment. Here was the old "African blasphemer," deferred to and honored by members of the Privy Council: the very man who, a lifetime earlier, had put Africans in the thumbscrew torture device to extract information from them about a shipboard plot to revolt. It was almost living proof of a line in a hymn which Cowper had written in 1773, and which Newton had published in 1774: "God moves in mysterious ways." A former slave captain was now poised to denounce the slave trade as sinful and wrong in front of the most august and influential body of British politicians. A former slave trader was ready to persuade the British government and people that the slave trade was a national sin.

In 1788 John Newton found himself center stage in the growing political drama about a trade in which he had prospered. He was now a famous man, and his hymns were acquiring growing popularity, and not only in Britain. They were soon to take root, three thousand miles away, in the fertile religious soil of North American worship.

"Amazing Grace" was just one of many hymns written by John Newton and designed to promote and explain a particular issue addressed in his weekly sermon before it became part of the *Olney Hymns,* in 1779. A year later "Amazing Grace" was chosen for use in the chapels of Lady Huntingdon's Connexion, a branch of Methodism that met initially in salons in her London homes, but later in various large-capacity chapels in central London. More important perhaps, in 1789 "Amazing Grace" crossed the Atlantic, when it was published in New York by members of the Dutch Reformed Church (centuries later to be supporters of apartheid). In 1793 it appeared in Virginia in a collection of hymns published by a Baptist preacher, and six years after that, in 1799, a Congregationalist minister published the hymn in Hartford, Connecticut.

Even before John Newton's death in 1807, though "Amazing Grace" had been published in a single English collection, it had appeared in *three* volumes in the infant US. From those small, local origins, seeds planted in the rich soil of North American Christian worship, there was to flourish the astonishing American attachment to "Amazing Grace."

Though the British affection for Newton's hymn increased in the course of the nineteenth century, when it was to be found in ever more hymnals, "Amazing Grace" remained only modestly popular in British worship. The fact that Americans took the hymn to their hearts while the British remained largely unmoved by it was sometimes put down to differences in matters of taste between the two countries. Some British critics even sniffily dismissed "Amazing Grace" as among Newton's poorer hymns. For all that, "Amazing Grace" quickly took root in a rapidly changing and expanding American society.

The people and cultures of the new republic were changing at a dizzying pace. It was a society founded in part by Christian refugees, where a wide variety of Christian churches flourished across the face of its urban and rural landscapes. Moreover, those early Americans of all backgrounds proclaimed their worship in song, in a fashion and with an intensity that surprised and sometimes alarmed European observers. Of course American music-making was not confined solely to worship at church. Americans everywhere could be heard singing: enjoying music at work, at home, in public places, and with friends. They sang and played music wherever they lived and worked, from the dockside of Atlantic ports to the slave gangs laboring on plantations on the very edge of settlement. This musical America was most famously captured by Walt Whitman on the eve of the Civil War.

> The carpenter singing his as he measures his plank or beam,
> The mason singing his as he makes ready for work, or leaves off work,
> The boatman singing what belongs to him in his boat, the deckhand singing on the steamboat deck,

The shoemaker singing as he sits on his bench, the hatter singing as he
  stands,
The wood-cutter's song, the ploughboy's on his way in the morning, or at
  noon intermission or at sundown,
The delicious singing of the mother, or of the young wife at work, or of
  the girl sewing or washing[21]

. . .

"Amazing Grace" arrived in North America at an opportune moment in
the story of church music. It was promptly incorporated into the hymnals of American churches, which were proliferating rapidly across
North America, and answered the growing demand for hymns to feed
the needs of rising American religiosity. It is true that the British birthplace of "Amazing Grace" also experienced a rise of new religious movements, with growing numbers of people, notably in the new industrial
and urban communities untouched by the established Church, flocking
to dissenting chapels. But what happened in Britain was a pale shadow
of the waves of religious fervor that swept across North America in the
nineteenth century.

THREE

Crossing the Atlantic

THE EARLY SETTLERS IN NORTH AMERICA, and the millions more who were to follow in later centuries, carried with them complex cultural habits that influenced everything from the way they spoke and cooked to the way they worshipped and sang. North America became a famous haven for Europe's religious refugees, and an extraordinary proliferation of places of worship sprouted across the face of the new colonies. By 1750 there were something like fifteen hundred congregations, overwhelmingly Protestant, with an average of ninety families in each.[1]

Churches were hugely important in colonial America. In such a vast and widely scattered agricultural society, a local church could become a focal point for social life and for the spread of information and news. Churches were important as the center of people's community life. But they were also different from their European counterparts. Many of them, notably Congregationalist and Presbyterian churches, developed their own distinctive revivalist customs, marked by outbursts of emotional fervor that "transformed sinners into saints." "Soul searching," promoted by enthusiastic ministers, offered the prospect of salvation for all and the possibility of everlasting joy in heaven.[2] Evangelical preachers promised their followers that any sinner could be drawn towards divine grace: the ultimate surrender to God, which would bring a sense of exciting freedom.

Such revivals tended to be local and small-scale until the 1730s and 1740s, when a new type of evangelical preacher, traveling enormous distances, brought people together in large revival movements. All this took place to the rapturous sound of hymn-singing. What gave revivalists extra power and geographic reach was the way religion had spread into popular print. Preachers spread their messages via the printed word, and colonial newspapers gave their activities major coverage. Their message was also carried by music and song, most famously among the Methodists and Baptists.

The Christian congregations of colonial America were largely segregated: while Black and Native American Christians were more present in North American churches than has been commonly recognized, most congregations were not racially mixed. It is true that in the North up to the early nineteenth century, there were some racially mixed churches and some white enslavers encouraged their Black slaves to attend church with them. Thereafter a more severe segregated world emerged in northern churches.[3] But in the slave colonies of the South, congregations were more strictly segregated. The growth of Black Christianity, via the work of missionaries and a small handful of slave owners, saw the rise of congregations among the enslaved, who worshipped apart from their white enslavers.

· · ·

Among the religious groups that formed the core of settlers in the New England colonies, "vocal music meant mostly the singing of psalms." They followed the biblical injunction "to sing praise unto the Lord."[4] These popular oral traditions of choral singing were, in time, reinforced by the rich and widespread publication of choral music. Early psalters were of course imported from Europe, but American clerics were quick to draft their own versions, which included printed instructions about what to sing—as well as *how* to sing and how to worship through song. Congregations usually had a preceptor who sang a psalm, line by line, and the congregation followed. This "lining out" system became a familiar and deeply entrenched feature of American choral singing. It was to be used, centuries later, at some of the great rock and folk concerts of the late twentieth century. Though it created some inevitable confusion and a great deal of musical discord, it nonetheless helped lay the foundations for the widespread and popular involvement in choral singing—especially among the illiterate.[5]

There was a great diversity in the way people sang in church and, understandably, it created unease among those preachers who sought choral conformity. By the mid-eighteenth century, a number of American preachers had issued a variety of publications intended to lay down rules about what was deemed appropriate for proper choral singing. The growth of singing schools led by "singing masters" encouraged a rudimentary musical notation, and gradually a form of simple musical literacy took hold in the American colonies. The spread of printed music in the second half of the eighteenth century, allied to the arrival of new immigrants, along with new forms of music from Europe, helped to spread a rich musical and choral culture in the colonies. British hymns and psalms were among the notable imports and were to make their own impact in the late eighteenth century. Despite the growth of such printed materials, many people, especially in smaller, isolated communities, clung to the more archaic ways of singing.

. . .

Methodists were famous for hymn-singing and it proved vital in the transformation of religion in both North America and Britain. In North America hymns found both a new voice and an extraordinary popular following and energy. From the first, early Methodists "were taught to sing their faith and their theology." John Wesley, when sailing to America in the company of Moravians, had been greatly impressed by their hymn-singing "as a corporate expression of faith."[6] He even learned German to be able to translate their hymns, and included some in his *Collection of Psalms and Hymns,* published in 1737. A year later, another volume of hymns and psalms marked the formal origins of the Methodist movement.[7]

In America, Wesley's hymns were sung at open-air gatherings with the intention of attracting a congregation—proof of "the essentially social nature of religion."[8] But even Wesley's influence paled when compared to the astonishing impact of George Whitefield. This charismatic man with his magnificent voice and elaborate gestures quickly won over huge crowds of converts in communal outbursts of religious ecstasy, notably in 1739 on his preaching tour in Britain, which he aimed especially at the laboring poor.

Whitefield also grasped the importance of publicity to attract a crowd to his preaching. Even before he landed in North America in 1739, colonial newspapers told of his British success and the power of his oratory. Large crowds—upwards of fifteen thousand people—flocked to his American sermons. Whitefield became the main inspiration behind the Great Awakening in North America in the years 1739–41. He, and American printers, understood the power of the printed word. The Great Awakening was "perhaps the first great public event in the colonies that was mediated by, and to some degree created by print." Whitefield's sermons flew off the presses in Philadelphia and Boston, and newspapers were filled with news about Whitefield and his work. Printers—most famously Benjamin Franklin—realized there was money to be made both from Whitefield's events and from the remarkable demand for religious literature in general. Franklin wrote: "It seemed as if all the world was growing Religious: so that one could not walk thro' the Town in the Evening without Hearing Psalms sung in different Families of our every Street." Franklin the printer made the most of it: "No books are in Request but those of Piety and Devotion: and instead of Songs and Ballads, the People are every where entertaining themselves with Psalms, Hymns and Spiritual Songs."[9] This demand for religious literature helped secure Franklin's printing prosperity. His edition of John Wesley's *Hymns* was especially lucrative.

Though based in Philadelphia, George Whitefield traveled from Maine to Georgia, establishing himself as a celebrity—the first of his kind in North America. His evangelical oratory even won over the hardnosed rationalism of Benjamin Franklin, not to Whitefield's faith but to an admiration of Whitefield's hold over ordinary people. Together, the two men helped propel "the print revolution in the colonies." By 1745 "at least eighty thousand copies of Whitefield's publications had been printed in North America: one for every eleven American colonists."[10]

It was this climate of vibrant and excited North American religiosity and song that John Newton encountered when he stepped ashore from his slave ship in Charleston in 1749. He naturally made himself familiar with how locals worshipped and was especially impressed, though also confused, by a local dissenting preacher.[11] Eight years later, when both Newton and Whitefield were back in England, Newton began his dogged pursuit of Whitefield. He wrote to him with theological queries and rose before dawn to join the many thousands keen to hear him preach in London and Liverpool. Newton was impressed and elated. He especially liked the way Whitefield "made many little intervals for singing hymns—I believe nearly twenty in all." When they finally met, it was Whitefield's turn to be impressed, realizing he had, in John Newton, encountered a significant figure and a serious theologian.[12]

. . .

By midcentury, colonial America was a collection of prospering settlements. Largely rural, with the economies of its southernmost communities thriving on the backs of enslaved African Americans, it was also an astonishingly religious society. And as they worshipped, Americans sang. When "Amazing Grace" arrived in North America, it was launched into a new world that was already enthusiastic about and widely committed to singing hymns.

FOUR

America, Music, and "Amazing Grace"

NORTH AMERICA WAS MADE for "Amazing Grace," and indeed for any number of other similar hymns. Its American publication was part of a flourishing publishing industry devoted to religious material. At first, however, it was just one more imported hymn that became part of North American musical culture and part of a unique American pattern of musical instruction. Large numbers of Americans were taught how to follow music as they learned to sing hymns, thus acquiring a simple form of musical literacy. But imported hymns were merely one element of a remarkable musical culture that flourished across North America. The sounds, words, and rhythms of all the immigrant people—free and enslaved—mingled with the traditional music-making of various Indigenous people in all corners of the Americas.

From their first encounters, Europeans were struck by the music they heard among local Indian people on both sides of the continent. Spaniards in New Mexico in 1540–41 described Pueblo women grinding corn while singing to music played by a man "playing on a fife." Forty years later, Francis Drake, exploring the San Francisco Bay area, met the Coast Miwok, who "took such pleasure in our singing of psalms." In return, the locals sang and danced for the Europeans. On the other side of the continent, in the seventeenth century, Captain John Smith's account of his experiences among the Powhatan people in Virginia told similar stories of Indian music and dance, accompanied by drums and rattles. It made, he claimed "such a terrible noise as would rather affright, than delight any man." When they worshipped, the Powhatans sang and

✣✣✣✣✣✣✣✣✣✣✣✣✣✣✣✣✣✣✣✣✣✣✣✣✣✣✣✣✣✣✣✣✣✣✣✣✣

I. CHRONICLES.

HYMN XLI.

Faith's review and expectation.
Chap. xvii. 16, 17.

1 A Mazing grace! (how fweet the found)
   That fav'd a wretch like me!
I once was loft, but now am found,
Was blind, but now I fee.

D 3   2 'Twas

FIGURE 4. The first published version of "Amazing Grace." From John Newton, "Hymn XLI," *Olney Hymns in Three Books* (London: W. Oliver, 1779). By permission of Trustees of Cowper and Newton Museum, Olney, Buckinghamshire.

danced for upwards of five hours—one man clapping "as if he would keep time."[1]

For their part, European settlers arrived in the Americas with both oral and printed versions of their own musical cultures. Indeed, the early world of North American print was effectively driven by religious material. Puritan New England—the Bible Commonwealth—was home to a Calvinist theocracy and was also the birthplace of North American print culture.[2] At first, books were imported from London, but in 1640 the first book published in the English-speaking colonies was, significantly, *The Bay Psalm Book*. It was the start, in North America, of a pattern already established in Europe by Protestant reformers, of turning the psalms of David "into rhymed poetry with four-line verses," which were then "sung to a few popular tunes everybody knew." Here was the pattern that established the subsequent development of choral music in North American music for centuries.[3] Singing, especially religious singing, quickly became a major feature of American life. Americans sang at home, in churches, in public spaces, and at work. Samuel Sewall (one of the justices who sentenced twenty people to death at the Salem Witch trials of 1692) regularly commented on the ubiquitous presence of music. For twenty-four years he "set the tune" for the congregation at the Old South Church in Boston. At home, after dinner, his family and friends sang psalms and, of course they sang at church. Sewall's life was punctuated by music.[4]

By the early eighteenth century, however, the New England godly were worried about the decline in the *quality* of psalm singing, hence the spread of "singing schools." These were staffed by itinerant musicians who traveled from town to town holding evening classes. This work laid the foundations for a musically literate population in New England. To cater to this new musical culture, the first colonial tune books were published, with the aim of imposing a sense of order on choral singing—and moving away from what critics viewed as the chaos of the old "lining out" way of singing. Printed tune books were in effect codified rule books, showing congregations and informal singing groups *how* to sing psalms. The Reverend Cotton Mather, another key figure in the Salem trials, was especially keen to curb undisciplined singing—especially among the young. They should "Learn to SING and become able to sing by RULE, and keep to the NOTES of the TUNES, which our Spiritual Songs are set unto." His hope was to see that a new generation "Learn the proper Tunes."[5] He wanted an end to the kind of music described by the Reverend Thomas Walter in 1721 as "miserably tortured, and twisted, and quavered . . . a horrid Medly of confused and disorderly Noises."[6]

As it did in Europe, church music in colonial North America ran parallel with a rich tradition of popular folk music. This oral musical tradition, including popular ballads, flourished, though often to the great disapproval of the devout, notably because of its influence on the young. At the upper reaches of colonial social life, newly emerged American elites created their own patterns of musical entertainment, both at home and in the public sphere. Among laborers, free white and Black Americans sang as they worked—as did enslaved Black Americans at work in the brutal tasks of plantation life. From the enslaved in the rice fields of South Carolina, to wealthy Bostonians enjoying musical soirees, Americans of all types were well known for their enjoyment of music. We know this because colonial newspapers, diarists, and visitors provide us with rich evidence about the ubiquity of music in colonial America. The major towns were alive with musical events, from cheap fiddlers in taverns to costly concerts in Boston. Musical instruments were on sale in local shops, alongside sheet music and psalm and hymn-books, while peripatetic music teachers advertised their services in local newspapers, and others set up schools to teach music, dance, and some-times languages.[7]

This great variety of musical activity could be found in all corners of colonial America and formed a kaleidoscopic musical culture that wel-comed and absorbed the music of newcomers from all corners. The end result was that the music of America constantly enriched itself by accept-ing—by changing and adapting—new forms of musical life from all sorts and conditions of people, and from all corners of the Atlantic world. It incorporated music from across both Europe and Africa. "Amazing Grace" was to find a natural home in this rich, welcoming, and ever-changing American musical culture.

Despite the reluctance of many churchmen, "Amazing Grace" found a natural home in a multitude of hymnbooks published in the nine-teenth and twentieth centuries, though the world of print provides only one clue to its popularity. Like so many other aspects of popular musical culture, and popular culture in general, print tells only a part of the story. Even so, what happened in the world of print forms a crucial entrée to the history of "Amazing Grace."

The fortunes of "Amazing Grace" in the nineteenth century differed markedly on either side of the Atlantic. In its British birthplace, it was a hymn that remained marginal to local worship. It never gained the criti-cal or popular acceptance in Britain that it so quickly acquired in the US. Though the *Olney Hymns* were reprinted forty times in the nine-teenth century, "Amazing Grace" often failed to find a place in the major hymnbooks that dominated British worship. The hymnbook I used as choirboy in an Anglican church between 1948 and 1959 did not include "Amazing Grace." Even today, my own copy of *Hymns Ancient and Modern* (a popular volume that went through twenty-four editions between 1983 and 2012) does not include that hymn, though John Newton's work is well represented by other hymns. Though the hymn was to become hugely popular in Britain after 1970—as it did in the wider world—it took a long time to garner the musical or critical support in Britain the way it did in the US. Today British worshippers from a variety of denominations name "Amazing Grace" as one of their most popular hymns, but it was to take two centuries before "Amazing Grace" achieved that popularity.[8]

Throughout much of the nineteenth and twentieth centuries, the British, unlike the Americans, failed to warm to "Amazing Grace." Scholarly theologians and clerics in particular have been distinctly unenthusiastic about "Amazing Grace." The most prominent British hymnologist of the nineteenth century, whose lifetime study of hymns was published in London in 1907, pronounced "Amazing Grace" to be "far from being a good example of Newton's work." A recent scholar also felt that that judgment had "some justice."[9]

This transatlantic divide is also reflected in the history of the hymn's publication. Though it remained a minor feature of hymnology in Britain, in the US "Amazing Grace" became an inescapable presence in modern American hymnbooks. Hymnbooks were clearly important in the widespread American passion for hymn-singing, and in the very nature of American worship. Furthermore, they had an importance that went far beyond devotional life. Hymnals were published in enormous numbers by every Christian group, sect, and denomination and became an important factor in encouraging literacy and supporting family life, sociability, schooling, childhood experiences, private reflection—and even the growth of American poetry. The Second Great Awakening began in the 1790s in New England and transformed and reinvigorated the religious culture of North America. Hymnbooks became an essential feature of the resulting spread of religious fervor in North America. They were also published by any number of secular institutions: "benevolent societies, Sunday school unions, and even schools such as Samuel Phillips's Andover Academy published hundreds of thousands of copies." They were handed out as rewards, prizes, birthday mementos, and at graduations.[10] As a result, the hymnbook established itself an everyday feature of American domestic and social life and found a treasured place in American homes, in addition to churches and camp meetings.

Many editors of hymnbooks compiled and edited their volumes with particular audiences in mind. Often, the title was a clue. *Family Hymns* (1838) was prefaced by a sketch of a respectable family, at home, reading together. *Hymns for Mothers and Children* showed a similar image, of children gathered round their mother as she read to them. Other hymnals, following the tradition of Isaac Watts, used hymns as a means of teaching literacy to the young, which was thought to be vital if children were to read the word of God. Children likely turned to read their hymnbook when bored by the preacher at a church service.

During the Civil War, hymnbooks were even published for the battlefield. The Presbyterian Church in the Confederate States of America published fifteen thousand copies of a pocket-sized volume—*The Army Hymn-Book* (which included "Amazing Grace")—for distribution to mainly white, Confederate soldiers in combat. Alongside the Bible, hymnals in church enabled people who were unable to afford their own copies to read and to study. Commonly on sale at local general stores, hymnbooks were frequently given as gifts, and the new owner inscribed his or her name and the date on the inside pages, the pattern being repeated as the book passed from hand to hand down the generations. Any number of eminent American writers testified to the importance of hymnbooks in their lives. Indeed many nineteenth-century writers incorporated the presence of a hymnbook into their poems, novels, and stories. In addition, a multitude of contemporary illustrations that appear in nineteenth-century publications confirm the widespread presence of the American hymnbook in domestic and social life.[11]

The fundamental role of the hymnbook was of course in singing— both learning the words of the hymns and following the music—all within an increasingly literate society. The ubiquity of the hymnbook and its widespread use at home, in church, and in public gatherings shaped the personal and collective memory of hymn-singing. From early childhood through old age, countless numbers of Americans routinely picked up a hymnbook and acquired a lifetime's grasp of, and affection for, hymns. The US became a nation steeped in the culture of hymns and hymn-singing.

"Amazing Grace" was, then, just the latest addition to America's thriving musical culture. It was adopted primarily by worshippers, who were permanently welcoming to new hymns, whether written locally or imported from Europe. In this case, "Amazing Grace" was to become not only America's favorite hymn but also one of England's most durable and influential exports.

. . .

Although America adopted John Newton's words to "Amazing Grace," the music we know today as "Amazing Grace" was *not* the music that accompanied Newton's hymn in its early years in America. Though "Amazing Grace" had begun its English life in a hymnbook—the *Olney Hymns*—its American origin was in a tune book. Such books instructed the reader how to sing the music, not merely how to follow the words. They were produced as large volumes, each of which sometimes ran to hundreds of pages, and included both music and written text. Hymnbooks, by contrast, normally contained only the text of a hymn. In a tune book, a song was known by its tune, not by the title of the hymn text. These books had their origins in the late seventeenth century and were popular among the pioneering settlers in New England.

The importance of the tune book in the new American republic was established, above all, by the work of Andrew Law. Though based in Rhode Island, Law traveled extensively as a music teacher, all the while compiling tune books, the first in 1779. But in his book *The Musical Primer* (1802) he abandoned the traditional method of teaching musical notation and devised a new "shape note" system of musical instruction. Similar systems, using shapes to denote particular notes, had long been in use—but Law simplified it by reducing the system to a mere four shapes. Thus:

Square = fa
Oval = sol
Triangle = la
Diamond = mi

Others, notably William Little and William Smith, published a competing book of shape note instruction, *The Easy Instructor* (1801), which was hugely successful and went through numerous printings. The teaching of shape note music provided a system—in various forms and under different authorships—which enabled untold numbers of people to acquire a basic comprehension of musical notation. Its success can be measured by the fact that it survived into the twentieth century.

The books of instruction for shape note music, the teachers who used them, and the singers who learned their music in this fashion quickly spread through New York, Pennsylvania, the Shenandoah Valley, and the Ohio River Valley, then to the rural US South in the early nineteenth century.[12] From this flux of musical innovation, and its geographic diffusion across large tracts of the US, there evolved the music we now associate with "Amazing Grace," music that eventually *became* "Amazing Grace."

Collections of sacred tune books were published by a number of enterprising clerics and publishers, most of them using the shape note system. In the rural US South, a thriving folk music tradition drew on the work of early compilers of hymns and tune books, but also adapted anthems and folk tunes that were already familiar to the singers. The actual composers of much of this music were often unclear—not surprisingly since much of the music was simply swept up from existing oral musical traditions—with the compiler of the tune book often claiming authorship for himself. Each borrowed from earlier collections, incorporating new tunes they had encountered. Little attention was paid to the music's authorial origins. What mattered most was the way the music was to be performed.

In the shape note tradition, anyone could lead the singing, but "each song is supervised by a single individual." The outcome was usually very loud.[13] This shape note tradition gave pride of place to a dominant singer who was capable of leading the way, singing a line or a prompt, which others could then follow and join in. For all its simplicity, it was a remarkably influential form of musical instruction and practice, winning over countless churches and rural gatherings across the US South. It was much less successful in the Northeast because there it faced people—mainly Congregationalists and Presbyterians—who insisted on more formal hymn-singing, even though many of their tunes were similar.[14]

The expansion of folk singing in congregations, and at revivalist meetings in the South, was closely linked to this shape note movement. In addition, shape note publishing also became a major enterprise in the South, helping to establish a repertoire of songs and hymns that survived down to the present day— "Amazing Grace" prominent among them.[15] But because of the way the shape note tradition evolved, it is difficult, sometimes impossible, to precisely locate the origins of certain tunes. A number of hymns and sacred songs that became popular in the US in the nineteenth century via tune books owed their origins to this confused mingling of musical roots. It also explains why the musical origins of "Amazing Grace" have proved elusive.

It was long thought that the music for "Amazing Grace" originated in *Virginia Harmony,* a tune book published in Virginia in 1831. However, more recently discovered evidence for its origins lies in a tune book published in 1829 by Charles H. Spilman and Benjamin Shaw in Cincinnati, entitled *Columbian Harmony.* Most of the music they included had already appeared in earlier tune books, and the music of two of the hymns—"Gallaher" and "St. Mary's"—has a close similarity to the modern version of "Amazing Grace." Furthermore, both those hymns seem to have links to Irish and Scottish folk songs, and both Charles Spilman and Benjamin Shaw grew up in areas of important Irish and Scottish immigration. We also know that traditions of harmony singing were brought into backcountry areas of Pennsylvania, the Carolinas, Virginia,

Georgia, Tennessee, and Kentucky by British immigrants from Wales, Ireland, and Scotland.[16] What emerged as the music for "Amazing Grace" seems to have its origins in the blurred mix of immigrant folk music.

All this is uncertain. There is no doubt, however, that *Virginia Harmony* contained the music that is recognizable as today's "Amazing Grace." Yet here (and in other tune books of the 1830s), that music was *not* linked to the words written by John Newton, but was instead attached to other hymns. The wedding between today's music for "Amazing Grace" and John Newton's words took place only in 1835, more than sixty years after Newton first drafted the hymn.[17] And that was the work of William Walker (1809–1875). Known by the name "Singin' Billy," Walker was born to poor parents of Welsh ancestry and was raised in a Baptist church. He became a music teacher, traveling extensively throughout the South, using the shape note system of music teaching and acquiring an enviable reputation across the South and Southwest. He also collected music and songs from any available source, compiling them into various collections. In 1835 he published *The Southern Harmony and Musical Companion* (printed in New Haven, Connecticut), which was, according to the title page, "A Choice Collection of Tunes, Hymns, Psalms, Odes, and Anthems." It contained 209 songs, of which Walker claimed 29 as his own. It was to have a profound and lasting influence. As late as 1992 a southern rock group—the Black Crowes—used the title of Walker's tune book for the title of their own album.[18]

Walker had been assisted throughout this work by his brother-in-law Benjamin Franklin White. Both men were experienced music masters who worked across a wide area of the South, and both were alert to the region's songs, hymns, and the folk traditions. They were also very conscious of how much people enjoyed singing. Consequently they set out to assemble, in book form, music that people would enjoy and which would also promote the cause of religious music. According to Charles Hamm, *The Southern Harmony and Musical Companion* contained hymns, spiritual songs from New England, and a number of folk hymns found in early shape note collections and pieces, all refined by Walker "based on the melodic tradition of Anglo-Celtic oral-tradition music." By 1866, it had sold six hundred thousand copies. One of its 209 songs was "New Britain." In it, "the character of the melody permeates the entire composition."[19] The tune had already been published in earlier volumes, but Walker changed it, refined it, and renamed it "New Britain." He also attached to it John Newton's words for "Amazing Grace."

For more than six decades, Newton's words had been sung to a variety of other tunes, most of them unknown. In Britain for example, it had been published, in three editions between 1779 and 1820, to the tune "Hephzibah," by G. Husband.[20] Now, Walker's new arrangement, which linked Newton's words with the music "New Britain," created an utterly new formulation.[21] It formed the words and music we know as "Amazing Grace" today. The music and words came together as if they had been specifically designed for each other. Yet it had taken many years of chopping and changing, of aligning each side—the music and the words—with a variety of partners. Now, the two slid together, hand in glove. It was, in music biographer and critic Steve Turner's words, "a marriage made in heaven."[22]

During Walker's travels through the South, he had listened carefully to the music he encountered, always alert to local musical traditions, picking up pieces of music, songs, hymns, and folk songs and transcribing what he heard. It is to Walker's attentive curiosity about existing popular music that we owe the modern version of "Amazing Grace." Walker's work put together music that had uncertain and imprecise origins in the popular choral culture of southern immigrants and settlers and which, in time, became today's globally famous hymn. Students of American folk music claim the hymn as their own—a hymn rooted in American folk. According to one study of country music, "Amazing Grace" is "the best known folk-country hymn today."[23] Today, any number of country music artists sing "Amazing Grace" as part of their repertoire.

"Amazing Grace" quickly took its place in the formal world of printed music. Once published in *Southern Harmony,* it became an important element in the rapidly disseminated hymnology of American life. Henceforth, "Amazing Grace" was read, sung, followed, and learned by growing armies of American singers and worshippers. *The Southern Harmony and Musical Companion* became "perhaps the most popular tune book in the South before the Civil War."[24] In the process "Amazing Grace" became as American as apple pie. Even when *Southern Harmony* faded from use in the late nineteenth century, the tradition lived on of having a periodic *Southern Harmony* "sing." In Benton, Kentucky, an all-day "sing" has been held on the fourth Sunday in May each year since 1884.[25]

·   ·   ·

When Walker published *Southern Harmony,* he made no acknowledgment of his collaborator and brother-in-law, Benjamin Franklin White. White departed in a huff to work as a singing master in Georgia. And it was there that he produced "the most famous, most influential, and most enduring of all shape-note tune books." Published in 1844 in Philadelphia, *The Sacred Harp* was designed, according to White, "for all classes who sing, or desire to sing."[26] White devoted his life to encouraging a widespread love and understanding of music—especially among the poor. He sought "to teach them to sing such songs as would bring them in sacred nearness to their Maker."[27] *The Sacred Harp* made an incalculable contribution to American musical literacy and culture. Throughout the 1850s, fresh editions tumbled from the presses, and annual conventions (beginning with the Southern Musical Convention, started by White in 1845) attracted "singing-school teachers and their pupils" who would spend the entire day singing from White's book. A committee chaired by White supervised new editions of *The Sacred Harp.* Regional conventions broke away from the main annual convention and took root in Alabama, Arkansas, and Texas, all sponsoring and monitoring singing teachers, all using *The Sacred Harp,* and all holding annual "sings" in their home region.[28]

The Sacred Harp movement continued well into the twentieth century, with large annual conventions and regular new editions of the book itself. New songs and hymns were added both to the choral performances and to new editions of the book itself, many drafted by the latest editor or compiler. At the same time, in the Northeast, a "reformed" hymn movement maintained a fundamental dislike of many features of the southern movement. It dismissed the "trashy publications which supplied the churches, especially of the South and West." But it too used the shape note system to promote its own hymnals, one of which, *The Christian Minstrel,* first published in 1846, went through an astonishing 171 editions in the next thirty years.[29]

The durability of these shape note music publications in the US is amazing. One, *The Good Old Songs,* first published in Thornton, Arkansas, in 1913, had reached a twenty-second edition in 1960. That volume contained "763 pieces, [and] went through a printing of a million and a half copies." By then, 54.25 million copies of all editions had been printed.[30]

Here then was a form of musical instruction and musical enjoyment embraced by millions of people across the US into our own time. It enabled countless numbers of people to grasp and then explore musical notation. It was at its most forceful and influential among the devout and was used specifically to promote Christian worship through singing and choral enjoyment. But its consequences went far beyond church worship. Like literacy and numeracy, it gave a new kind of power to people who had traditionally been denied access to music. Musical literacy gave people a voice that could be heard clean across the land. It was to become an integral aspect of the remarkable musical culture that emerged in the US in the course of the nineteenth century, and in which "Amazing Grace" became a central item. Equally, John Newton's words were henceforth tied to the music that millions today know as "Amazing Grace." Forging the link between the words and the music had been slow and uncertain but "Amazing Grace" had at last taken on its recognizable modern form and sound.

FIVE

Music in Slavery and Freedom

"AMAZING GRACE" IS MUCH-LOVED in African American communities and a favorite hymn in Black churches, not least because its words, offering hope and the prospect of better things to come, seem ideally suited to the experiences of Black life in the US. It took little time for the hymn to establish itself as a prominent feature of the wider musical culture of African American life, a culture that was conceived and nurtured in the unforgiving history of slavery. By the late eighteenth century—by the time John Newton spoke to the Privy Council about the slave trade—there were some seven hundred thousand enslaved people living in North America, and millions more lived in Brazil and the Caribbean. By then, enslaved Africans worked in every conceivable job in the Americas, from the docksides of major ports to domestic service in the mansions of the wealthy. White observers recorded that wherever the enslaved lived and worked, they sang.

From the first days of European exploration of West Africa, white outsiders remarked that "Africans" seemed to them especially musical. It became a stereotype trotted out from that day to this and it was used to justify enslavement and exploitation. Thomas Jefferson's assertion that Africans "are more generally gifted than whites with accurate ears for tune and time" is typical of these claims.[1] Black musicality was also invoked by Black writers of the time, for example by the freed slave, merchant, and abolitionist Olaudah Equiano in his memoir of 1789: "We are almost a nation of dancers, musicians and poets."[2]

Throughout the enslaved Americas and Europe it was common to train the enslaved as musicians, and advertisements for their musical services are common in colonial newspapers. Both free and enslaved Black musicians were commonplace in Europe, where they were especially associated with the French horn. In 1757, an advertisement in a Bristol newspaper described a Black teenager who had escaped enslavement thus: "A NEGRO LAD about 18 years of Age, near five Feet two inches high answers to the name Starling, and blows the French Horn very well."[3] We also find evidence of Black musicians working on ships, serving in naval bands, in addition to performing for fashionable society. Equiano was perhaps the best-known example of an African who played a musical instrument: he even paid a neighbor in London to teach him to play the French horn.[4] Some free Black musicians attained recognition for composing in popular European styles, among them Ignatius Sancho, a prominent British African living in late eighteenth-century London, who wrote twelve musical pieces between 1767 and 1779 as well as a *Theory of Music*.[5]

Much more significant, however, Africans transplanted into the Americas their own music from their African homelands. Few Africans stepped ashore from the slave ships with any form of material possessions. We have numerous accounts of their naked, or near naked, condition on arrival. But they arrived with, in addition to the traumas of enslavement and transportation, a myriad of cultural assets: languages, foodways, beliefs—and their memories and experiences of life in Africa. They also carried the varied storytelling and music-making of Africa. All this evolved into a culture that flourished among the enslaved throughout the Americas. Much of the music played in the slave quarters had its roots in Africa, and for that very reason it was suspected and often feared by slave owners. What, for example, were white enslavers to make of slaves drumming or blowing on a conch shell, the sounds echoing great distances? Were the slaves sending messages among themselves—or merely enjoying a musical tradition foreign to European American ears? White churchmen were likewise suspicious of the music made by enslaved people, not least because, as one claimed in South Carolina,

Black "feasts, dances and merry Meetings" tended to take place on the Sabbath—inevitably, since for most that was their sole day of rest from labor.

But white observers were correct that the enslaved did sometimes use music as a form of subversion. Sometimes this was literal: in the Stono Rebellion, a large uprising of the enslaved in South Carolina in 1739, the rebels "halted in a field, and set to dancing, Singing and beating Drums, to draw more Negroes to them."[6] On other occasions, it took the form of asserting their right to the meaning, pleasure, and community that music can offer, in lives in which the most basic rights were denied to them. On holidays, when slave owners permitted, slaves gathered together on plantations, or for those laboring in towns, in fields nearby, to drink and sing at events that sometimes continued through the night. They made music with a variety of musical instruments, many similar to instruments played in Africa but made from materials available in America. This nascent Black musical culture naturally drew on a variety of African regional elements, all changed and blended by the conditions of life under slavery. We can see this in the musical instruments played by the enslaved, the most famous of which was the banjo. By the late eighteenth century, the banjo had become the centerpiece of Black music-making in North America.

Dancing—to the banjo, fiddle, and drums—was a universal feature of enslaved life. On festival days, it was commonplace for all sorts and conditions of white folks to join in. One white observer asserted that slaves would walk miles "to enjoy the pleasures of flinging about their hands and legs to the music of the banjo." There "he performs with astonishing ability, and the most vigorous exertions, keeping time and cadence, most exactly, with the music . . . until he exhausts himself."[7] White folks who joined in usually found it hard to keep up.

At dances, as the fiddler played, another slave would beat a drum, or simulate a drum with sticks or needles. Another would beat out the rhythm with his or her hands or feet. When the fiddler tired, others took over, beating out the rhythm by clapping or slapping their thighs. Solomon Northrup described this "patting" on a Louisiana plantation, with slaves "striking the hands on the knees, then striking the hands together, then striking the right shoulder with one hand, the left with the other—all the while keeping time with the feet, and singing." Sometimes a slave recited verses, "a shrill sing-song voice, keeping time to the measure . . . by beating her hands sometime against her sides, and patting the ground with her feet."[8]

The enslaved were regularly called on to play, sing, and dance for their enslavers. White people also "hired" particularly gifted enslaved musicians for more formal musical entertainments and dancing, paying the musicians' owners for use of their labor. George Washington for example paid Harry Piper twelve shillings for his "slave Charles playing the fiddle" at a ball in Alexandria.[9] The enslaved musician John Drayton was a brilliant fiddler, who "fair made the fiddle talk. When Master gave a dance he always calls upon John. Yes sir, that man could play." He was so good he could even "make a parson dance." The city of Charleston had a reputation for its "Negro Dances," parties held by slave owners at which enslaved dancers and musicians performed for white guests: "When our master had company, they would often collect all the slaves for a general frolic."[10] White Virginians in particular were renowned for their wild, enthusiastic dancing, "a practice originally borrowed, I am informed, from the Negroes." One slave owner "could shake a desperate foot at the fiddle" and was especially eye-catching when dancing "a Congo Minuet."[11]

This lively musical culture among the enslaved could be heard—and enjoyed—from the waterside of Atlantic ports to remote plantations and settlements in the interior; it thrived in the huddle of plantation huts and cabins and was on display in the grandest of planters' mansions, and in taverns in all the major cities of the colonial Americas from Williamsburg to Rio. Much more common and striking though was the music that enslaved people made when they worked.

Wherever slaves toiled, they sang, creating musical and choral rhythms intended to make the toil more tolerable. Oarsmen rowing a boat in South Carolina struck up "their plaintive African songs, in cadence with the oars."[12] One white passenger described being carried along by "a dozen stout negro rowers"; when the boat's leader sang a brief line, the others responded with synchronized oar and choral response. The words of their responses changed, ad-libbing, as they progressed, but always kept pace with the rhythm of the oars. The passenger recalled that their verses were by turns observant, sharp-witted, and vulgar—and the journey was paced to the flash of the oars and the choral response of the oarsmen.[13] The English actress Fanny Kemble described in 1838 how slave oarsmen "accompany the stroke of their oars with the sound of their voices. . . . The chorus strikes in with the burden [refrain] between each phase of the melody [which is] chanted by a single voice."[14]

Whatever the task—sawing, chopping, hammering, digging, rowing, husking, picking—slaves sang. Logging gangs paced their labor to musical chants, working in pairs as they felled Virginian timber for a railroad in the 1850s they sang, chopping in turns and singing as they swung the axe.[15] It was much the same among slaves reaping corn in Kentucky, moving through the wheat as a team, "swinging their brawny arms in unison as they cut the ripened grain, and moving with the regular cadence of the leader's song."[16]

From the multitude of slave work songs, perhaps the best remembered and best documented are those from the cotton fields in the first half of the nineteenth century, the years of King Cotton. By 1860 almost two and half million enslaved people lived in the US South, and workers in southern cotton fields produced some of the most memorable Black music. Picking cotton in the sweltering heat of the Delta imposed its own pace. One woman, explaining how she managed a grueling day of picking 150 pounds of cotton, said, "We would pick cotton and sing, pick and sing all day long."[17]

The enslaved thus marked the cycles and calendars of agricultural life in music: hog-killing, rice threshing, log-rolling, corn shucking, whatever the local agricultural activity, it took place to the sound of slave music. Favorite singers clambered on top of a pile of corn to serenade the crowd—free and enslaved. At one rice threshing, "the rhythmical beat of the numerous flails is accompanied by a recitative and improvised song of endless proportions, led by one musical voice, all [the slaves] joining in the chorus, and can be heard a mile."[18]

FIGURE 5. "Plantation Slave Singers," Virginia, 1840s. Illustration in Mary Ashton Rice Livermore, *The Story of My Life* (Hartford, 1897). Courtesy of *Slavery Images: A Visual Record of the African Slave Trade and Slave Life in the Early African Diaspora,* http://www.slaveryimages.org/s/slaveryimages/item/1005.

Some slave owners tasked a singer specifically to lead the workers in song. In fact, sensible slave owners recognized the value *to them* of permitting those they had enslaved to make music. The free time and pleasure enjoyed by the enslaved was useful to the slave owner: they expected slaves to return from it ready for work again. There were, for example, few cotton plantations without an enslaved fiddler: sometimes the owner favored him with special treatment, knowing that his Saturday night and Sunday music was essential to a better running of the property. "I buy the fiddle and encourage it," admitted one planter, "though some of my good old brethren in church would think hard of me."[19]

In the words of Frederick Douglass, "Slaves are generally expected to sing as well as to work. A silent slave is not liked by masters or overseers." The sound of slaves singing helped the boss locate where they were and confirm they were at work. When they received their food and clothing allowance, they made the land "for miles around" reverberate with "their wild notes." The musical culture of the enslaved could benefit their enslavers.

. . .

Singing was then an inescapable feature of slave life. There was often what Frederick Douglass called "a tinge of deep melancholy" to the music made by slaves. Revealingly, Douglass claimed he had "never heard any songs like this anywhere since I left slavery, except when in Ireland. There I heard the same wailing notes, and was much affected by them. It was during the famine of 1845–46."[20] From the fields and from the slave cabins, enslaved people created songs that told of coping with the bleak harshness of enslaved life by offering up personal and collective musical expressions of deep unhappiness.

Sometimes slaves could be heard singing in praise of their masters, offering their gratitude for what they received. Only the most deluded of slave owners took that at face value. It was sarcasm that masked resentment and hatred. Frederick Douglass saw the reality: "Every tune was a testimony against slavery and a prayer to God for deliverance from chains." It was, he thought, a grave mistake "to suppose them happy because they sing." On the contrary, "the songs of the slave represent the sorrows, rather than the joys of the heart. . . . Sorrow and desolation have their songs, as well as joy and peace. Slaves sing more to make themselves happy, than to express their happiness."[21]

Time and again, white observers noted that the music of the enslaved was quite unlike any to be heard among white people. Some tried to catch it, writing down the words and tunes, trying to capture what they heard. But it wasn't until 1867 that the first collection of slave songs was published, *Slave Songs of the United States*. Eventually six hundred slave songs were collected (at much the same time that European folk songs were being collected). These truly African American songs had roots in Africa, were shaped by the experiences of transportation and the brute realities of American slavery, and were blended with European and sometimes Indigenous peoples' music.[22]

· · ·

The most haunting songs from the slave quarters were those about the destruction of family life. The enforced removal of loved ones was a permanent threat and reality for all slaves, and it left deep abiding scars throughout the history of slavery. At a stroke, people were removed from their loved ones and sold—disappearing over the horizon forever, leaving behind grieving and lamentation, as well as songs that carried the pain down the generations. January 1—a traditional day for slave auctions— became known as Heartbreak Day.[23] When enslaved people were forcibly driven away—sometimes trekking huge distances to a new property, often chained two by two—they sang "wild hymns and mournful melody." This was the unspeakable misery suffered by enslaved Americans— almost one million of them in the years 1790–1860 alone.

In the caravans that drove enslaved people from the Upper South to the Deep South, slaves were sometimes forced to sing and dance in their rest periods; much the same had happened to Africans on the Atlantic slave ships. If there was a musician in the traveling group, he was expected to play as others danced or sang. Solomon Northrup's skill as a fiddler was used in this fashion. Northrup, a shrewd guide to the world of slave music—born of his own experiences—wrote that music "was my companion—the friend of my bosom—triumphing loudly when I was joyful, and uttering its soft, melodious consolations when I was sad." At night, his music "would sing me a song of peace." It soothed his aches— especially on the Sabbath.[24]

. . .

Here then was a rich musical culture that was deeply embedded among the enslaved people of North America. For legions of slaves, music and music-making had long been a feature of their working, family, and social lives. Slaves sang at family and communal ceremonies, at funerals, at weddings—and at all those festivals of the Christian year. As the enslaved converted to Christian worship, they were inevitably won over to the music of Christian worship—*but on their terms*. Among enslaved people, the music of Christian worship joined already well-established musical traditions and expressions. Church and chapel music were just the latest form of musical culture taken up by America's enslaved

FIGURE 6. "Meeting in the African Church, Cincinnati, Ohio," *Illustrated London News,*
April 30, 1853. Library of Congress, LC-USZ62-30794.

population. Long accustomed to their own styles of singing and music-
making, the enslaved easily adopted Christian musical worship that fitted easily into the ways they already enjoyed music. White missionaries
and iterant preachers were delighted to discover that slaves were "remarkable for learning a tune" and were impressed by the quality of their
hymn-singing.[25]

Hymns and psalms were ideally suited to the existing musical culture
of North America created by slaves, and this was true in other slave societies across the Americas. Slaves were especially attracted to the "lining-
out" of hymns and psalms, in which a preacher or choral leader "recited
or 'called' a stanza of a psalm or song and led the congregation in a sung
response."[26]

The voices of slaves were increasingly raised in Christian worship.
"Along with the Bible, Watts hymns were among the first books given to

blacks."[27] Many slave owners feared slave literacy and after Nat Turner's Rebellion in 1831 it was made punishable by law across most of the South. Prior to that, some enslavers had offered slaves access to hymnbooks during white church services; in slaves' "own meetings they often made up their own words and tunes. They said their songs had more religion than those in the books."[28] Even so the existing hymnbook literature offered a rich source of comfort and hope: it spoke of suffering and redemption, of pain and salvation, of sin and grace. Often however, hymns meant something quite different to the enslaved than to their owners. The Bible and hymns offered hope for people looking for a better life and for an end to life's ordeals.

> O Canaan, sweet Canaan
> I am bound for the land of Canaan.

To slaves, this might have meant not only heaven, but also an earthly destination: the North and freedom.[29] In the songs that slaves adopted or crafted, biblical references sometimes pointed *not only* to heavenly aspirations, but to more immediate and mundane hopes: of freedom and peace in a world beyond slavery—somewhere far away from the plantations—along the dangerous routes that led north to freedom. Thanks to the Lord's amazing grace, they sang, there were better things to come.

> Thro' many dangers, toils, and snares
> We have already come
> 'Twas grace has brought us safe thus far
> And Grace will lead us home

It was as if John Newton had been writing with the enslaved in mind. His poignant words had a meaning far beyond the parish bounds of Olney in England. They chimed wherever the enslaved in the Americas heard them, adopted them, and sang them. Not surprisingly, "Amazing Grace" became a favorite slave hymn.

. . .

The music created by the enslaved laid the foundations for the astonishing rise of the rich and varied African American musical world in the days of freedom. By the late nineteenth century, the music of African American musicians and performers, had become a seminal element in the rise of a massive US entertainment industry. Of all the different kinds of music that characterized America's musical culture, the best remembered and perhaps the most influential was that which emerged from the US South. Music that had its roots in Africa emerged, via the slave quarters, to influence first the US then the wider world.

All the miseries and all the hopes and expectations of enslaved people were registered in the rich miscellany of slave music. Emancipation in 1866 was followed by the punitive racism during Reconstruction and as the descendants of freed people began to move away from the South, they carried that music with them. The Great Migration saw African Americans quit the South in droves, starting in the 1910s, heading for the major urban areas of the North, the Midwest, and the West Coast. This migration transformed the human face of the US. In 1890, 90 percent of the nation's African American population lived in the rural South. A century later that had fallen to just over half. The waves of migrating African Americans transplanted the musical cultures conceived in slavery and nurtured in the hard days of the Civil War and emancipation, right across the US. In the process, they laid the foundations for the extraordinary blossoming of Black musical talent in the US in the years before World War I.

The musical talent and interests of African Americans, and indeed the types of music they had nurtured, largely hidden from the outside world in slave days, now found new ways of expressing themselves and making a much wider impact in the US at large. Touring Black musical groups, choirs, individual musical stars, composers, and a host of Black musical entrepreneurs emerged in the late nineteenth century as public entertainers and successful commercial artistes. New types of music—the blues, jazz, honky-tonk, gospel, and others—followed in the wake of people leaving the South, and they revealed the great variety of Black musical talent as never before. Much of that music, but especially the

B. W. THOMAS.   F. J. LOUDIN. H. D. ALEXANDER.   THOMAS RUTLING.
MAGGIE L. PORTER.   JENNIE JACKSON.
JULIA JACKSON   ELLA SHEPPARD.   GEORGIA GORDON.   AMERICA W. ROBINSON.

FIGURE 7. The Fisk Jubilee Singers formed in 1871 to raise money for the new Fisk University in Nashville. The group became hugely popular in the US and Europe. Unknown photographer, 1875. National Portrait Gallery, Smithsonian Institution, NPG.2002.92.

blues, was steeped in and reflected the racist oppression and poverty of African American life in the South.[30] But now, in the late century, it was to be seen and heard in every conceivable public space in the US, from street corners and town squares, through to local theaters, bars, bordellos, and even major concert halls. Black choirs, singers, and musicians performed before enormous crowds at all of America's major jubilees and national anniversaries, all in addition to untold numbers of amateur and part-time African American musicians who touted their musical wares from barbershops to local street corners.[31]

Best remembered perhaps were the Black choirs that became a prominent feature of late-century US musical life. The most celebrated were the Fisk Jubilee Singers, formed initially to raise money for the new Fisk University in Nashville. By 1872 they were famous, singing to huge crowds across the US. In Europe, they introduced tens of thousands, including some of the crowned heads of Europe, to the "folk music of black America." Other Black choirs followed their lead, opening the eyes of the wider world to the world of Black music.[32]

Black minstrel groups, for instance, toured the US and Europe; the more successful groups often advertising their performances by parading through the town to whet the local appetite. Minstrelsy, which began as a derisive mockery of Blackness by white performers wearing blackface, opened to Black performers after the Civil War and eventually became a major entertainment industry, one of the few to employ thousands of African Americans; it had its own specialist columns in major newspapers. Famous musical stars emerged from these minstrel troupes, some establishing themselves as singing stars in their own right. Eventually, the world of minstrelsy was absorbed into the expanding world of vaudeville and into major Broadway musical productions. But its major songs, performers, and acts lived on well into the twentieth century.[33] Other African American singers and musicians had successful careers in the more formal world of America's concert halls, though black female singers were more readily accepted than their male counterparts: talented male singers tended to drift into choirs or touring groups to pursue their musical careers.

The most obvious link between music-making in slavery and in the days of freedom—one that thrives to the present day—was the world of sacred and church music. Emancipation and the end of the Civil War were followed by the explosive growth of African American churches. No longer under the controlling and usually suspicious eyes of slave owners, emancipated people across the US South were now largely free to worship as they wished. Though they were often in danger of being attacked, hundreds of new churches sprang up, many with a Methodist or Baptist affiliation and most gradually associating themselves with national or annual gatherings. It was at those major gatherings and conventions that the most notable form of African American church music—gospel music—evolved. Smaller religious groups regularly broke away from the larger denominations to establish new, independent churches, notably Holiness churches, where music and dance with clear links to an African past were at their most striking. And like churches everywhere, African American churches needed hymnbooks.

The first African American hymnbooks had appeared in the bleak years of slavery when Black political leaders and preachers, both in slave and free Black communities, asserted their claims to equality both at worship and in society at large. They placed great value on having their own hymnbooks. In the words of Christopher N. Phillips, "The production of a hymnbook was among the first official acts by community leaders to say to themselves and the world: we are now a people."[34] Many of the well-established forms of communal worship in Black communities grew out of African musical traditions, blended with the Christianity of their enslavers. The spread of African American Christianity developed new forms of musical worship characterized by choral, revivalist singing, often expressing an enthusiasm that was markedly different from other churches. In particular, the revivalist element in African American Christianity, like its white equivalent, was awash with the sounds and excitement disliked by more traditional worshippers, Black and white. As a result, many leaders of early African American churches sought to distance themselves and their followers from what they viewed as the excesses of revivalist faith and music.

In 1817 the African Methodist Episcopal Church—AME in Philadelphia—published its *Discipline,* a "set of principles for using a hymnbook to ensure right worship." This was followed, a year later, by *The African Methodist Pocket Hymn Book.* Leaders of the church, worried about ensuring the formality of worship, tried to insist on the selection of appropriate hymns, demanding that congregations should *not* sing "hymns of your own composing." Yet at the same time, congregations were urged "to retain the spirit of singing."[35] Hymns were compiled and published that seemed best suited to each congregation, and thus it was that individual churches and church organizations began to publish their own hymnbooks.

Years before, John Wesley had been angered when American Methodists produced their own hymnals, even when they included some of his hymns. But such local editions were part of the process of imposing a *discipline* on worship: part of the effort to curb excessive revivalism. In order to assert the respectability of local worship, editors of African American hymnbooks were determined to keep revivalist hymns and singing out of church worship. Yet revivalist hymns lay at the very heart of the way many African Americans worshipped outside the formal boundaries of local churches.

"Amazing Grace" established itself as a favorite in revivalist singing in the nineteenth century and for that very reason, it was usually *excluded* from African American hymnbooks throughout much of the century. There are few examples of "Amazing Grace" among the mountains of hymnbooks. But this does not mean that "Amazing Grace" was not popular or that it was not sung. As with the world of folk songs and popular culture in general, the real story of popular hymns is not primarily to be found in the world of printed hymnals. Though "Amazing Grace" was not included in many early hymnbooks, there is a wealth of information to show that it had been a popular hymn among slaves, most of whom, in any case, were illiterate. Former slaves, interviewed deep in their old age by researchers from the Federal Writers' Project in the 1930s, recounted stories of how hymns were sung—and how they were remembered. Jim Davis—then aged ninety-eight—from Pine Bluff, Arkansas, recalled his banjo-playing in slave days:

> I used to be a banjo picker in Civil War times. I could pick a church hymn just as good as I could pick a reel. Some of them I used to pick was 'Amazing Grace'. . . . I could pick anything.

> Amazing Grace
> How sweet it sounds
> To save a wretch like me.[36]

Slave children picked up hymns at Sunday school or church. Pete Newton from Clark County, Arkansas, interviewed at age eighty-three, reported, "I learnt to sing the hymns but never sang in the choir." Katie Rye, also eighty-three, looked back to the time when "we sang the old hymns and 'Dixie.'"[37] Old people recalled childhood memories of camp meetings in the South. They would listen to a preacher, "then we'd sing some more such as 'Amazing Grace, how sweet the sound, that saved a wretch like me.'" Nick Waller told how he worshipped in Athens, Georgia: "Folks had religion then and from the time the pastor read out the song and the brother in the corner started it off, everybody would 'gin to git happy and when that old song 'Amazing Grace. How Sweet the Sound' was sung, the shouting could be heard for a mighty way off."[38] It was precisely this kind of ecstatic church singing that was frowned upon by outsiders, and which many church leaders took great pains to prevent. Hence the tight control over the nature and contents of hymnbooks. We need then, to be aware: the huge volume of nineteenth-century hymnbooks can sometimes hide as much as it reveals.

. . .

The sheer volume of American hymnals published in the nineteenth century is remarkable. The most prodigious editors spent a lifetime devoted to the cause. Lowell Mason, for example, in a career spanning fifty years, edited twenty such volumes, one of which sold half a million copies. Another, Thomas Hastings, "composed six hundred and more than a thousand hymn tunes and published fifty volumes of music."[39] Most editors of church volumes wanted a tight form of choral discipline, and their reluctance to include revivalist hymns in African American hymnbooks explains the absence of "Amazing Grace" from many of those volumes. The hymn did not appear in AME hymnbooks until 1890. Indeed the only black church to include it prior to that (in its hymnbook of 1829) was the Union Church, a church that had a more liberal approach to revivalist hymns in general. Yet at the same time the Baptist and Presbyterian churches included "Amazing Grace" in *all* their major hymnbooks by the 1840s. The irony remains that African American hymn collections were ambivalent about "Amazing Grace"— not because the hymn was unpopular but because of concerns about how the church would be viewed by outside critics.[40]

. . .

Church leaders faced an intractable problem posed by the popularity and strength of oral musical traditions. Large numbers of worshippers who enjoyed hymn-singing and who had sung together for years had no need of hymnbooks to guide or instruct them. This, after a fashion, was the tradition of singing at the camp meeting. People who could not read or understand basic musical notation simply sang as they liked. They picked up tunes and the accompanying words from those around them and from a lead singer. The hymns they liked and sang tended to be simple, with a verse-chorus format, allowing singers to join in the chorus. This pattern of choral singing had been evolved by African Americans, most notably in the call-and-response of slave work songs. It was relatively easy to adapt such singing to hymns sung in church. One person would sing the basic verse or text: the rest of the congregation or crowd would join in and follow. A century later, this form of singing was widely used in the protest songs of the Civil Rights movement.[41] And it lives on, to this day. It was precisely this formula that President Obama employed to rouse a choral response with "Amazing Grace" in 2015 at the College of Charleston. The president knew what he was doing: he realized that he was prompting a congregation long accustomed to responding to a lead singer's promptings. Uniquely, in this case the prompt came from the president of the United States.

SIX

Singing and the World of Print

AMERICAN HYMNOLOGY OF THE NINETEENTH CENTURY, like American worship at large, was suffused with the theme of salvation. Salvation was a powerful, haunting refrain regularly invoked by preachers at camp meetings and at massive revival gatherings especially in the late nineteenth century. Time and again, hymns—and the preachers who promoted them—told their congregations and gatherings that sinners could be saved. Whatever their sins, however sinful their past, the repentant could be saved. Few hymns captured this simple point more clearly than "Amazing Grace." Salvation lay at the heart of "Amazing Grace," and despite the various alterations made to Newton's verses in a number of American editions, the basic message—of salvation—survived. As "Amazing Grace" was absorbed into America's religious and musical life, and as its verses appeared in one hymnal after another, the music that accompanied those verses changed. It is important to remind ourselves that for many years, Americans—and others—did not always sing "Amazing Grace" as we sing it today. Nor were the verses always the same. Along with other hymns, both the music and the verses of "Amazing Grace" were changed according to the tastes of successive editors and compilers of hymnbooks.

. . .

"Amazing Grace" arrived in North America at an opportune moment, when there was a growing demand for hymnbooks to feed rising American religiosity. In the 1820s and 1830s the Second Great Awakening opened religion to mass involvement, with the almost irresistible appeal to common folk—not merely to the "elect"—that they too could determine their own destiny.[1] It was carried along by waves of evangelical Protestantism, notably among Baptists and Methodists, and driven by a number of powerful and highly emotive preachers at large revival meetings. Huge numbers of people were converted to the cause, as the Awakening spread out from its early base among groups in Kentucky and Tennessee, with men on horseback taking the message to receptive, eager crowds. Enormous crowds gathered at camp meetings, often in places with no established church or chapel. The Second Great Awakening spawned schools and colleges, reshaped groups and movements, and supported a wide range of reform issues, from Temperance to abolition. Throughout the 1820s and 1830s, monthlong revival meetings were held across the US: they seemed to be proof, in many people's eyes, that here was a movement which was purifying the nation. It was an awakening that persuaded untold numbers of people to confess and to abandon their sinful ways.

Above all, it was a movement that helped to establish the US as a deeply Christian nation, and this was reflected in massive growth in church membership. In 1776 there had been a mere two thousand Christian clerics in the new nation, a population of almost four million. Fifty years later that had risen to an estimated forty thousand clerics for a population of seventeen million, of whom one million were Methodists.[2] Naturally, there was much more to this Second Great Awakening than simple numbers. It was, most striking of all, a *democratic* movement that attracted all sorts and conditions of people—all ages and social ranks, rich and poor, men and women, free and enslaved—to crowd into revivalist meetings. And it was there, in public, that they confessed and abandoned their sinful ways and committed themselves to more godly lives. Preachers told their huge audiences that each person was a free agent, free to choose between a sinful or a religious life. Once they opted for that new life, they could earn God's grace.

This astonishing upsurge in American religiosity was also propelled, and in many respects made possible by, the material changes in American life. Preachers traveled not only on horseback but also, increasingly, on railroads and steamboats, their expensive travels paid for by funds raised at their massive revivalist meetings. Moreover, the preachers' religious messages were not only *heard* by the people packed into those crowds, but also *read,* thanks to a massive proliferation of printed material. As ever more Americans became literate, they acquired great volumes of printed matter: sermons, lectures, tracts, psalms, and hymns. Churches and chapels became not only centers for worship, but also nodal points for the spread of literacy. Worshippers were encouraged, through formal classes and informal help, to read the Bible as well as the tracts distributed by preachers and organizers. They also read the hymns, which were available in the enormous hymnbooks that spilled from the new mechanical printing presses and were distributed quickly and cheaply across the nation. Worship and singing from hymnbooks went hand in hand.

The Second Great Awakening also established Christianity on the American "frontier" and in areas remote from white population centers. There, local people camped out in advance of a revival meeting, singing and praying as they waited. Sometimes the crowds swelled to their thousands. An estimated four hundred such camp meetings were held in 1811 alone. Such gatherings were especially attractive to African Americans, many of whom staked out their own "shouting-ground" within the meetings, while many others attended the general meetings as equal participants in worship. For Black and white to join in religious worship as spiritual equals was a rare phenomenon in a society dominated by slavery. Many critics, especially clerics, railed against the kind of singing that emerged from such gatherings: they disliked the enthusiasm and vigor of the singing, dismissing the "merry airs" that were "often miserable as poetry" and "senseless as matter." One of the most severe critics, John F. Watson, a Wesleyan minister, disliked the fact that such hymns "were most frequently composed and first sung by the illiterate blacks of the society."[3] Worse, in Watson's eyes, Black attendees even *danced* to the hymns, sometime singing one hymn after another without interruption. It seemed to such critics to be a disjointed music, stitched together from field work, folk songs, and scraps of formal hymnology. Worshippers stomped, clapped, exclaimed, shuffled, and gyrated. It was a form of Christian choral worship that seemed at variance with everything Watson and many like him regarded as the true way of worship.

Here was religion and worship that was loud, musical, and exciting, which allowed worshippers the "freedom to sing as they saw fit." Sometimes, it continued throughout the entire night.[4] Many of those involved could not read. But that did not matter because they sang in the way traditional folk songs were sung around the world. Worshippers sang "short, simple statements of music and text, with plenty of repetition and redundancy."[5] People added verses as they went along, developing a form of singing that many white observers recognized from listening to the enslaved at work. And all this was taking place alongside the expanding publication of printed hymnbooks.

American camp meetings were, in effect, a totally new form of Christian worship. For a start, they were so huge that no contemporary buildings could hold them: they *had* to take place in the open. Equally, because of their size, they were noisy: people congregated over a large area and needed to hear what was being said, sung, and prayed. They were also meetings that attracted an unusually wide spectrum of American churches and sects and needed a common religious element to appeal to all comers. Equally, whatever was sung had to be simple and repetitive. A stanza had to be uncomplicated and brief, something that could be repeated chorally when attached to a refrain.[6]

The most prominent—the loudest and most ecstatic—singers at camp meetings were reported to be Black Americans. One Swedish visitor described them as "a magnificent choir." At one gathering of seven thousand people in 1838, another visitor noted that "their shouts and singing were so very boisterous that the singing of the white congregation was often completely drowned." Some white church fathers, including the Methodist John H. Watson, disapproved of their singing sacred songs "in the merry chorus-manner of the southern harvest fields, or husking frolic method." They added verses of their own to the hymns.

Choruses were also added, developing into "wandering verses" that were popular at camp meetings.[7]

Many worshippers at camp meetings were, of course, illiterate and had no explicit instruction in music. But the ability to follow and to pick up a tune did not require such formalities, any more than workers in field crews needed songbooks to acquire and follow work songs. What they *did* need however was a choral prompt—a note, a phrase, a line (ideally crisp and easily followed)—which they could copy and join in.

This American choral tradition of the early nineteenth century marched in step with a flurry of publications designed for use by music masters and aimed at promoting instruction of simple music reading. As chapter 4 explored, the shape note system, known as the "fasola" system, became basic to the way music was taught in the growing number of singing and music schools and classes throughout North America.[8] Shape note publications were often dismissed by critics, however, as cribs—dunce notes—for dim country people. Yet it was a system with enormous importance in the spread of musical learning and choral activity across the US in the nineteenth century.[9]

When we bring together these two phenomena—the vitality of widespread, popular choral traditions at camp meetings, and the development of formal singing via tune books and hymnbooks—we can see the emergence of a popular and widespread American musical culture. It is hard to overstate the importance of the nineteenth-century camp meetings in the development of this culture. Moreover, many scholars agree that at its heart lay the African experience, transplanted into a Western Protestant culture before being adopted, in its turn, by white worshippers. Camp meetings became a place of cultural fusion, perhaps like no other in North America, where Black and white came together to create a uniquely North American cultural expression: a distinctive American voice and sound.

Outsiders were in no doubt that the loudest, most enthusiastic singing at camp meetings came from Black people—enslaved and freed. They sometimes sang long into the night. "At half-past five . . . the hymns of the Negroes, which had continued through the night, were still to be heard on all sides."[10] In time, Black musical culture absorbed "Amazing Grace" and transformed it from a simple hymn from the depths of rural England into an American and then a global anthem.

. . .

This widespread passion for choral music was an important element in the armory of any number of the American evangelists who rose to prominence later in the nineteenth century. These Christian preachers wooed and won over huge crowds to their preaching and to the choral involvement at their meetings. Two men in particular, Dwight L. Moody and Ira D. Sankey, stand out for their impact in both the US and Britain and for their success in attracting huge late-century crowds to their meetings. One of their converts thought they had "reduced the population of hell by a million souls."[11] The prospect of salvation, which they dangled before their audiences, proved very persuasive—and had been used by John Newton himself in letters, sermons, and hymns a century earlier.

Like other evangelicals, Moody sought to bring the gospel to the ungodly of the US, not by fire and brimstone, but by gentle and effective persuasion. As Moody preached, Sankey played and sang what became known as "gospel songs." Invited to Britain by British evangelicals, Moody appealed to local ministers of all denominations, and they, in turn, urged parishioners to attend Moody's gatherings, where Sankey served as musical director. Despite fierce opposition from some quarters, they were hugely successful, especially in Scotland, where they inspired a national revival.[12]

Sankey's music-making and singing, which had been honed in the Methodist world of Pennsylvania, and Moody's preaching formed a potent combination that had already lured vast crowds to their evangelical gatherings in the US. In Britain—after a poor start in York—they repeated their American successes, attracting astonishing crowds. People were regularly turned away from their overcrowded venues.[13] Like Newton a century before, Sankey and Moody believed that music was a key to winning over a crowd. They were also masters of modern publicity, coaxing the press, making effective use of advertisements, and rallying famous names as well as humble folks to their cause.

They worked hard at their campaigns, setting themselves a relentless personal timetable. In Britain, for example, their two days in Manchester were packed from morning to night. On Tuesday, December 22, 1873, they performed—and it was a performance—at the Free Trade Hall in Manchester, with a "PRAYER MEETING at twelve noon: BIBLE READING at three p.m. EVANGELISTIC MEETING at 7.30pm. Wednesday same as today."[14]

Their down-to-earth style filled the largest of city venues wherever they appeared. They held 285 such meetings in London alone. Theirs was a style which, inevitably, was heartily disliked by the more solemn corners of British worship. When Ira Sankey performed in the parish church in the small Derbyshire town of Chapel-en-le-Frith, one parishioner was so outraged that he thought the local bishop "will have something to say" to the curate who had invited him.[15]

Throughout, Moody portrayed Christ himself as a sinner, a person with whom armies of ordinary people could identify. If Christ could be saved, so too could the humble and ordinary people in the audience. Salvation was there for all. This simple, seductive point, a potent message for the poor in the late nineteenth century, was exactly what John Newton himself had pressed home, in his letters and hymns a century before. Salvation was available to all who repented.

Moody preached in a comforting, unadorned style that immediately elicited a personal response from the audience, whatever its size. Sankey's musical style was similarly humble and affecting. Equally important perhaps, he sang hymns that were direct, simple, and catchy: songs he had gathered together and that stood in sharp contrast to many of the traditional hymns his English contemporaries were accustomed to singing in their local churches and chapels. In style and substance, Sankey's songs were new and fresh to his English audience. They were also *relevant* to people's lives, and made sense in ways that traditional hymns did not. At a gathering in Sunderland, the local vicar described Sankey's vocal work as "singing the gospel." The phrase stuck—both to Sankey and to his style of religious music. People rushed to buy copies of the "gospel songs" that Sankey and Moody subsequently published under their joint editorship.[16] Their collected hymns sold vast numbers, and each edition grew longer than the one before.

After Moody and Sankey's return to the US from Britain in 1875, their revivalist work swept across the US, at every turn carrying with it a huge output of published hymns and religious songs. They also inspired other American evangelists in the late nineteenth century, many of whom adopted their habit of recruiting an established singer to accompany them. What emerged was an important school of preachers who made effective use of both music and song. For most of them, as for Moody and Sankey, the core of their missionary work was the question of salvation. Many, perhaps most, of the gospel songs they used have faded from memory, but the most popular "have become woven into America's musical consciousness" and have endured in the most popular of hymn collections.[17] "Amazing Grace" was among the most popular.

British audiences had wanted printed copies of what they had heard at the meetings, and Sankey rushed out an early cheap pamphlet, *Sacred Songs and Solos*. It consisted of a mere twenty-three songs and cost only a few pence. It sold an estimated 3.5 million copies. When he returned to the US, Sankey worked in alliance with Philip Bliss on a more substantial edition. Bliss was an experienced music salesman who also had a fine singing voice, and he was persuaded to lend his voice and charismatic presence to Moody's evangelical cause. Sankey and Bliss jointly produced *Gospel Hymns and Sacred Songs* in 1876, followed by a second volume, *Gospel Hymns 2*, published for a campaign in Boston in 1877. The latter included, for the first time, "Amazing Grace"—but the music attached to the words, "Warwick," was not the music we know today. The next volume, *Sacred Songs and Solos,* published in the US in 1879 and in London in 1880, also included "Amazing Grace," this time with yet different music ("Claremont"). *Sacred Songs and Solos* was regularly revised. By 1906, it contained some twelve hundred items.[18] Between 1870 and 1902, Sankey produced an astonishing thirty different collections of hymns and sacred songs.[19] There was serious money to be made from successful editions of hymns. Sankey and Bliss's *Gospel Hymns and Sacred Songs* of 1876 yielded royalties of $360,000 in the first ten years, and the proceeds were funneled back into their ministry.[20]

The revivalist meetings initiated by Moody and Sankey, and followed by many other, less famous preachers, spread across the South and North, both in cities and rural areas. Many of the gospel songs they published were closely linked to traditional folk music, and by the end of the century, this gospel music had penetrated even to the remotest of communities.[21] The hymns they used were now "heard and sung in virtually every part of America, penetrating to even the most remote corners of the land."[22] However, more prosperous folks tended to shy away from such religious fervor and outbursts, preferring to worship and follow their faith in quieter, more traditional fashions.

· · ·

The gospel music that became an integral aspect of African American churches and their communities was thus paralleled by a related form of gospel music that evolved among white worshippers, primarily in rural southern churches. It was at its most strident and vocal in Louisiana. Though both Black and white gospel music thrived in Pentecostal churches from the late nineteenth century onwards, it was later to find its modern home in the evangelical movement, which emerged in the late twentieth century.

White gospel had originated in the shape note music and Sacred Harp singing that flourished across the South in the early twentieth century.[23] Prominent among its proponents was Beylus Benjamin ("B.B.") McKinney, whose *Broadman Hymnal* (1940) was issued both in shape note and conventional musical notation and became the standard songbook for Baptists in the South. Better known still was James Houston ("Jimmie") Davis, twice elected governor of Louisiana, who made his name as a country music singer. His compositions and recordings from the 1920s to the 1950s helped promote and popularize white gospel music, and rural southerners came to regard their gospel music as an aspect of their broader culture, which also involved a dogged attachment to segregation. Later, white gospel music became an element in the conservative evangelical Christianity that became such a force in late twentieth-century American politics.[24]

The importance of shape note singing in the development of white gospel music was amply confirmed by the research and publications of George Pullen Jackson. A professor of German at Vanderbilt University, Jackson was an indefatigable researcher who documented and recorded the extensive culture of shape note singing in the South. Published as *White Spirituals in the Southern Uplands* in 1933, his findings had an impact on a number of contemporary composers, notably Aaron Copeland and Ruth Crawford Seeger (the stepmother of folk singer Pete Seeger). In 1936, Jackson discussed a version of "Amazing Grace" that he had encountered and that had been "ornamented"—that is, the music had been slightly altered from the original. It was, he thought, "an excellent illustration of the widespread southern folk-manner of singing hymns of this sort."[25]

In general, however, southern white gospel music went largely unnoticed by scholars. But the findings of a small band of devoted researchers, led by the father-and-son team of John and Alan Lomax (working for the Library of Congress) and Jackson, explored and documented white gospel, confirming its existence as an important living musical tradition among scores of white communities and churches across the US South. The popularity of "Amazing Grace" in that musical culture was to be an important element in the transformation of "Amazing Grace" in the late twentieth century.

. . .

During the years of late nineteenth-century US revivalism, incalculable numbers of hymnals and gospel songs tumbled off the presses on both sides of the Atlantic. Many of them included "Amazing Grace," though most did not list the hymn under that title.[26] Nor did they attach it to the music we know today. In these publications, it appeared as a hymn based on John Newton's original wording, though often with new stanzas added. Sometimes compilers even added their own verses: in *Uncle Tom's Cabin*, Harriet Beecher Stowe has Uncle Tom sing "Amazing Grace" with the addition of a new stanza of her own composition.[27] Ira Sankey's important innovation was to include "Amazing Grace" in his collection *not merely* by number or by the name of the music (which had been the previous pattern in publications) but under the title "Amazing Grace." By 1890, "Amazing Grace" was securely embedded in Sankey's *Sacred Songs and Solos,* "the defining hymn collection of late-nineteenth-century Evangelicalism."[28] In the early years of the new century, the hymn was to be elevated to a different level, thanks to the work of yet another major American hymn-writer and evangelist singer, Edwin Othello ("E. O.") Excell.

Born into a German background, Excell's early life was that of a laborer and builder: he left that to become a music teacher before finding work with a number of prominent evangelists. Today, Excell (1851–1921) is regarded as the last of the old school of singing evangelists, with a voice that spanned the nineteenth and twentieth centuries. He was a remarkable singer, who could sing both baritone or tenor with unusual range and tone, and he was capable of attracting tens of thousands to his performances. A man of great physical strength and industry, as his strenuous preaching and singing career progressed, he wrote and published more than two thousand hymns. He had a remarkable ability to create choirs from groups of people who had never sung before. He was also a shrewd businessman and, starting in 1881, formed his own publishing company for religious material, editing some fifty volumes of hymns of his own and helping with the publication of many more. In time, sales of these works exceeded one million copies a year. Excell naturally profited from this prodigious output. When he died in 1922, he left in the region of three hundred thousand dollars: in today's terms, about $4.8 million. There was clearly good money to be had from catering to Americans' love of religious music. It should not diminish Excell's faith, nor that of others like him, to note that the riches created by American religious music were a forerunner of what was to unfold in the late twentieth century when the global entertainment industry generated fortunes on the back of "Amazing Grace."

Excell was important in the history of "Amazing Grace": he remodeled it and give it a modern shape. When he included it in a number of his hymn collections, he stripped the verses down to a basic four (Newton had written six) and he changed the melody. In *Make His Praise Glorious* (1900), Excell included "Amazing Grace" and used the music "New Britain," listing the hymn as number 23. It was number 282 in his volume *Coronation Hymns* of 1910.[29]

Excell's version of "Amazing Grace" in *Coronation Hymns* was copied by editors and compilers of later volumes of hymns. Gradually the older melodies that had been used to sing "Amazing Grace" faded from use. Thanks to Excell's influence, the music "New Britain" became the standard music to accompany "Amazing Grace." These changes to the verses and the music—that is, the creation of a standard, widely accepted modern version of "Amazing Grace"—emerged primarily because of the power and influence wielded by Excell in the world of American religious music. His dominance as editor and publisher effectively reshaped and relaunched "Amazing Grace."

Excell's version of "Amazing Grace" was soon propagated by another dominant preacher of the early twentieth century. Robert E. Coleman, yet another prolific compiler of hymns, took Excell's by then standard text and had it adopted by the influential Southern Baptist Convention. Coleman, like Excell, was also a publisher of hymnbooks and songbooks, selling huge numbers to churches and church organizations throughout the South. By 1945 his company was the largest publisher of songbooks in the US.

The commercial successes of Robert H. Coleman and E. O. Excell provide striking examples of the lucrative nature of religious publishing in the US in the nineteenth and twentieth centuries. Religion was big business and, if marketed properly, hymns sold well. There was an enormous and apparently ever-expanding market of American consumers keen to get their hands on the latest hymnbooks. But none were to sell quite as well as "Amazing Grace" itself would in the late twentieth century. At the heart of this story of "Amazing Grace" in early twentieth-century America lay the work of E. O. Excell. His editing, his choice of music, and his commercial sway over contemporary religious music, allied to his power and influence as a publisher and as a guiding influence on many other editors and preachers, essentially guaranteed a special place for *his* version of "Amazing Grace." In the early twentieth century, "Amazing Grace" was being sung by congregations and conventions across the US, thanks in large measure to the hymnbooks published by Excell. It was the version we recognize today.

SEVEN

Musical Entertainments

VISITORS TO THE US in the early twentieth century were frequently struck by the all-pervasive presence of music. People sang, played, and danced to an enormous variety of music. They worked to it; they worshipped to it; they played it, sang it, and entertained with it at home; they even traveled to the sound of music. Descendants of the enslaved sang at work, and what was to become the blues and jazz filled their evenings and spare time. In the most isolated of communities—in Appalachia and in harsh settlements in the West—old ballads and cowboy songs, respectively, provided a musical life in the vastness of those lonely American landscapes. Each and every immigrant group on the East and West Coasts played and sang its own traditional music. And in the nation's booming cities, new commercial industries churned out unprecedented volumes of popular music. All this blended into a musical mix that seemed to define America itself. No one doubted that the US had become "a singing nation . . . and song was the vessel into which many Americans poured their greatest hopes and fears."[1] The US was, quite simply, a very musical place.

The tens of thousands of hymnbooks published, sold, or distributed free in the US in the nineteenth century formed, then, just one strand in America's musical culture. It was a culture that ranged from the simplest (though amazingly noisy) camp meetings through to finely tuned commercial offerings in theaters and concert halls in the nation's major towns and cities. Less obvious—but perhaps equally important—was the presence of music in the home, notably in the form of the piano.

Initially, pianos were imported from Europe and they were expensive. Starting in the 1820s, the US began to manufacture its own pianos, and rising American prosperity after midcentury enabled ever-more American homes to acquire them (alongside printed sheet music), eventually on a staggering scale.[2] The piano came to hold pride of place in the domestic musical culture of millions of Americans.

The price of American pianos fell by half between 1850 and 1900. In 1870 American manufacturers were producing some 24,000 pianos a year: forty years later that stood at 370,000. In 1910, when US manufacturers were producing more than 333,300 pianos a year, 1 American in 252 bought a new piano. American domestic music-making was now centered on the piano ("the household's altar") accompanied by an abundance of printed sheet music, which itself had been transformed by new print technology and distribution.[3] As production costs fell, enormous volumes of sheet music flowed out to flood the US market. The piano also created a new social role for many American women, offering them an opportunity for musical expression. Female pianists and vocalists emerged, inside the home and at public performances. Years later, female singers were to transform "Amazing Grace" from a much-loved simple hymn into a global commercial hit.

Among America's most popular songs in the mid-nineteenth century was "The Parlor Song." It and songs like it were sentimental, maudlin even; death and dying figured prominently, as did religious themes. They were in some respects a byproduct of the Civil War. Few families had escaped the painful consequences and trauma of that conflict, and for decades afterwards people found solace and comfort in music infused with sentimentality and pathos. It was often difficult to distinguish between religiously tinged popular songs and hymns. The line between popular music and sacred music was unclear and blurred—a pattern that would be followed in the late twentieth century when "Amazing Grace" was transformed from a popular hymn into a massively popular musical hit.[4] And both stories hinged on an aggressive commercial music industry.

. . .

As the US developed into an industrial and economic colossus, it underwent a revolution in its consumer culture, with music central to that culture. The rising consumer power of an expanding population transformed every aspect of music, and new commercial interests converted the public's appetite for music into profitable business. From the most sophisticated of theatrical and concert performances, to music-making in the home, music became a commercial cornucopia that had its commercial and creative center in New York City. Millions of Americans listened to music: they played and sang at home, they joined choirs and played in bands, so that "a town without its brass band is as much in need of sympathy as a church without a choir."[5] They sang at home, in public, in choirs, and at work. They paid to listen to music in theaters, at concerts, and in bars; they bought musical instruments and sheet music for the home. And, of course, they also worshipped to the sound of music. In churches, chapels, and open-air gatherings, Americans sang their devotional prayers, psalms, and hymns. As they did so, most of them held one of the popular hymnals. "Amazing Grace" regularly appeared in those hymnals.[6] From hymnals to sheet music, from classical concerts to barroom pianists, music in the US had become big business by the early twentieth century.

"Amazing Grace" would become an astonishing moneymaker in the late twentieth century. Its myriad recordings, multimillion record sales, and later its video and digital formats all generated money on an astonishing scale. It projected some performers to stardom. Yet it was only a simple hymn, written for parochial use: it was not designed for commercial success, but it became a moneymaking machine, the latest in a long list of musical successes in the world of American entertainment. After a fashion, "Amazing Grace" had already been part of a bestselling business in the late nineteenth century—in the form of the edited hymns that sold so well for evangelical publishers like E. O. Excell.

The modern US music industry has its immediate roots in the nineteenth century. One notable feature was the development of modern printed sheet music, which heralded a major change in the public's relationship with music. Effectively for the first time, music was now being written simply for the purpose of making money. But to write a bestselling song, writers realized they had to create simple, easily sung, and easily remembered tunes and words. They promptly churned them out in their thousands. Their songs were repeated endlessly, from coast to coast, in theaters and on vaudeville stages, and at public entertainments. Audiences quickly picked up the tune and the words of the latest popular song—much as people had learned hymns and psalms at worship over the past two centuries. Simplicity and repetition were vital.[7] This was precisely the pattern that had established the grassroots popularity of "Amazing Grace."

American commercial music changed dramatically in the late nineteenth century, courtesy of a new generation of music publishers and writers, many of them immigrants from Germany and Eastern Europe, and concentrated increasingly in Manhattan. Many of them had worked in other industries and knew how to sell commercial commodities. But they also grasped that to be popular a song had to become ubiquitous and inescapable. Thus Tin Pan Alley was born. It was originally located on 28th Street, between 5th and 6th Avenues, and rapidly become a massive industry in its own right and confirmed that "there was money in popular song."[8]

. . .

This world of American popular music was totally transformed by the impact of recorded sound and the new technologies of broadcasting in the early twentieth century. When brought together, recorded music and radio heralded the start of a massive cultural change. Its immediate consequence was the rapid decline of sheet music and the piano. After 1920, songs became popular not via printed sheet music and live performances, but via recordings and radio broadcasts.

At first it was thought that the player-piano (also known as the automatic piano or pianola, which created music mechanically) was *the* major technological innovation; between 1919 and 1925, US production of player-pianos outstripped those of conventional pianos. Even major pianists felt obliged to perform in public on the player piano. But its popularity was short-lived and it was soon rendered pointless by records and then by radio.[9]

Guglielmo Marconi's early experiments with wireless telegraphy were critical, but it was the pressing demands of warfare between 1914 and 1918 that hastened the rapid development of radio. Before 1914 there had been thousands of amateur radio fans scattered across the US, all busily experimenting with radio, despite a law of 1912 that tried to control radio interests by granting broadcasting licenses. By 1917 there were an estimated 13,581 licensed operators, and perhaps 150,000 unlicensed stations. Imaginative pioneers, local radio clubs, and commercial interests all realized the enormous potential of radio. Early efforts were often beamed within a very small radius, or even to a specific target (a hotel for example), and much of the broadcasting time consisted of music. This amateur passion for radio, at first curtailed when the US entered the First World War in 1917, was then boosted by the increased number of people skilled at working in military radio systems. When they returned to postwar civilian life, they were keen to renew their interest in radio—but now they were equipped with the latest technological knowledge, acquired in the military. Major corporations grasped the commercial potential of radio and began to manufacture equipment to sell to an eager US public. Between 1920 and 1922 a "broadcasting boom" swept the US.[10]

Early radio sets were simple and looked crude, but manufacturers were soon turning out radio sets that were attractive items of domestic furnishing, further hastening the decline of the piano as the centerpiece of the home. The appeal of radio lay of course in the content of its programs, brought directly into the home, and by 1926 radio stations across the US reported that music provided far and away their most popular programs—though not everyone liked what they heard. One American critic complained that in the home and on the street corner, there was hardly "any escape for the musically-timid."[11]

Meanwhile, recorded music emerged as an offshoot of the telegraph and telephone, and by the early 1920s new techniques had begun to iron out the crudities of early-century recordings. By 1929, the US was pressing more than 105 million records a year and manufacturing more than 750,000 phonographs, valued at almost $100 million. In that same year, 50 million records were sold in Britain and 30 million in Germany. Equally huge record sales in the same period could be found in countries as different as Finland and Peru.[12]

The invention of recording equipment—bulky, crude, difficult to transport and use—now enabled researchers to capture the sounds and voices of popular folk music. The pioneers who embarked on those early recordings in the US quickly discovered and recorded various examples of "Amazing Grace." Those recordings enable us to listen to the vernacular forms of "Amazing Grace" from the early years of the twentieth century, though their roots reach back to the popular folk culture of the nineteenth century. It soon became clear in the early years of the twentieth century that "Amazing Grace" was popular in a variety of US communities. We know this because it took little time for musical researchers and critics to discover Americans singing "Amazing Grace." It was sung in church, at home, and at folk gatherings in the remotest of locations. It was most audible and ubiquitous wherever African Americans came together to worship. It thrived as a popular song in the folk traditions of America, though at the time many feared folk music was in danger of dying out.

Such worries about the future of folk music prompted efforts to find and capture as much of it as possible: to locate it, then record it on the new recording equipment. Under the guidance of the Library of Congress, John Lomax and his son Alan set out from 1928 in search of the folk songs and ballads of the South. They recorded what they discovered and, in the process, they encountered "Amazing Grace" in widely dispersed locations. They heard it sung by young and old, Black and white. An elderly couple sang it for them in their Medina, Texas, home. The Lomaxes recorded a version sung by African American cousins in Livingston, Alabama, and by a fifty-five-year-old white female labor activist in Kentucky's Appalachian Mountains.[13] Thanks largely to such efforts to capture these voices, we have a wide range of recordings of "Amazing Grace": from Tennessee, Georgia, Kentucky, Alabama,

Louisiana, the Carolinas, and elsewhere. Today, many of these traditional versions survive in the holdings of the Library of Congress in Washington, DC, and some subsequently became available on niche recordings.[14] These researches in the late 1920s and early 1930s revealed that "Amazing Grace" continued to be sung to a variety of different tunes. Listening to them, it becomes clear that the version we know today had not yet taken hold fully at the grass roots of US music-making. Isolated communities and singers continued to sing "Amazing Grace" much as they had since time out of mind; in their own way, to music fashioned as they saw fit, and largely unaffected by the trend to sing it to "New Britain." The full commitment to "New Britain" would have to wait for the full impact of recorded and broadcast music a little later. Before then, in the words of one singer, many continued to sing "Amazing Grace" to "the tune I first knew in my childhood."[15]

Community worship and folk singing had been the most universal forms of passing on worship and musical tradition. They required neither formal learning nor musical literacy. Later, the rise of formal worship in churches, chapels, and camp meetings imposed a different structure and strength on musical worship. Then recorded music, especially via the radio, utterly transformed both worship and the popularity of religious music. Songs now became popular via the airwaves. Old songs and hymns could, in an instant, reach millions of people via radio. In the US, the whole process was accentuated by the parallel emergence of gospel choirs and powerful gospel singers. Henceforth, and down to the present day, simple hymns that had been written solely with an eye to local, specific congregations—a small group of people gathered in a particular church—could now be projected to audiences measured in their millions. Legions of ordinary folk began to lend their own voices to hymns that had, not long before, been the preserve of relatively small groups of worshippers. The people's voice was raised in communal praise and worship, adding an often thunderous and tumultuous sound to the way people worshipped.

. . .

The Library of Congress researchers revealed the remarkable degree to which "Amazing Grace" lived on in vernacular music-making. It was also just one example of a flexible process of popular culture at work: a blending of hymns printed in hymnals, with old folk traditions expressed through a variety of melodies. The result was that "different communities all across the country adapted 'Amazing Grace' as needed."[16]

It was clear enough in the early twentieth century that "Amazing Grace" was deeply embedded, and widely popular, in the folk music of the US quite apart from its more formal presence in African American churches and chapels. Not surprisingly, it took its place on what was to become perhaps the center stage of American country music. Nashville's Grand Old Opry began life in 1925 as a radio program. One of the first performers was Herman Crook. When interviewed towards the end of his life, "Herman brought out his harp [harmonica], and gave me a concert of some of the old songs he used to play in the show in those days." He included "Amazing Grace."[17]

. . .

These early recordings also confirmed that that there was no hard and fast demarcation between folk and church music. "Amazing Grace" seeped from one genre to another. It was heard and adopted by people wherever John and Alan Lomax undertook their investigations, and it was sung from childhood to old age. No one particular group owned or claimed "Amazing Grace" as their own. Lee Hays (later to become a prominent folk singer and the man who introduced Pete Seeger to "Amazing Grace") first heard "Amazing Grace" as a boy in Little Rock, Arkansas, both at his father's Methodist church and in local African American churches. Hays was influential in bringing the song to the attention of a new generation of folk music fans.[18] He was one conduit through which "Amazing Grace" moved from church to folk venues. If we bring together the different strands of "Amazing Grace," that is, both the presence of "Amazing Grace" in African American churches and its popularity as an American folk song, we can begin to understand the remarkable resilience and popularity of "Amazing Grace" long before it acquired its post-1970 global fame.

. . .

Throughout the 1920s, commercial radio in the US relied heavily on music for programming, usually performed by bands and orchestra playing from studios or hotels. From the start, the major radio companies appreciated that "music was extremely effective at building an audience."[19] Musicians and singers now became famous simply by performing on radio, sidestepping the traditional route to popularity via stage performances. The musical repertoires of early radio programs were very familiar to audiences because radio reprised the songs and music produced by established music publishers in Tin Pan Alley.[20]

Radio swiftly ushered in a cultural revolution in the US in the 1920s; between January and December 1922, the number of licensed radio stations increased from 28 to 570.[21] Radio sets quickly replaced the piano, first in prosperous homes, and later, as the cost of radio sets fell, in low-income homes. Americans poured their money into radio sets: $60 million in 1922, rising to $136 million in 1924.[22] In 1923 there were 190,000 radio sets in American homes; six years later that had risen to 5 million—when the population stood at 123 million.[23]

This story of American radio and of recorded music was part of the much broader story of rising American prosperity. By the end of the 1920s, one half of American families owned a car. Cinema-going doubled in that decade. To acquire tempting consumer durables, Americans borrowed money. The nineteenth-century virtues "of thrift and self-denial" had given way to immediate gratification and mass consumption.[24] But all was brought to a juddering halt after 1929 with the onset of the Great Depression, though by then the cultural patterns of the 1920s were unshakably rooted in American life. Music filled the airwaves and had become the background sound to everyday urban life. Today, we are accustomed to the inescapability of music of all kinds in almost every public place. This "musical landscape" was first established—at astonishing speed—in the 1920s. The record industry, new radio stations, and the development of electrical loudspeakers beamed musical offerings into most corners of urban US life (and most Americans lived in urban areas). It was as if music had entered the nation's bloodstream. It was so pervasive—so influential—that major industrialists and academics began to study ways music might be used to commercial ends. If music cheered, encouraged, and sustained listeners, might it not be useful in promoting industry, hard work—or relaxation—and all with a commercial purpose?

. . .

By 1927, one quarter of all US homes had a radio set. A year later, broadcasting became national via sixty-nine NBC radio affiliates spanning the entire continent. Listeners could now tune in to an unprecedented variety of music on the radio, from classical to folk, and from nearly all corners and ethnic groups within the US.[25] Radio united the nation. The most remote of places, small towns scattered across the vastness of the nation, and isolated one from the other, were now linked—by radio. Observers were rhapsodic: "How fine is the texture of the web that radio is even now spinning! It is achieving the task of making us feel together, think together, live together."[26]

Radio brought together, as never before, the peoples of the US, scattered across its vast landmass. It was now possible to entertain the entire nation—simultaneously. It was also possible to take *specific* musical cultures—hillbilly, western, Appalachian, African American, immigrant music of all sorts—and bring them into an American musical mainstream.

Early listeners were in awe of being able to adjust their radio dial and lock on to distant stations. They could also *choose* what they wanted to hear, and all in the comfort of their own home. One music fan in Philadelphia returned his ticket for local concerts, preferring instead to listen to the same concerts at home. Radio's potential seemed vast, though the reality of broadcasting was more mundane. Optimists, hoping to see the elevation of American taste by the broadcasting of "good" music, were quickly disappointed. Though concerts, opera, and major solo artistes regularly appeared on radio, the airwaves were dominated not by "serious" music, but by a wide range of popular music. And some people complained about it. It was the start of a complaint about popular music that continues to this day.[27]

Popular music on the radio became an unavoidable presence. If you patiently tuned your radio dial, it was possible to receive every type of music played throughout the US. With the arrival of religious broadcasting, it was also possible to enjoy hymns, choral, and sacred music, again in the comfort of your own home. Before radio, music had been a face-to-face experience: listening to or watching musicians and singers perform, or singing and performing oneself. Now, music could be enjoyed anywhere there was a radio set and a signal. Today, the ubiquity and global presence of music is so obvious—so much a part of the modern world—that we take it for granted. But this universal reach and impact of music was ushered in, very quickly, with the advent of radio. In the words of the preeminent historian of US broadcasting, "this unprecedented turn to music listening constituted an enormous perceptual and cultural realignment that reshaped the twentieth century."[28] People, of course, had sung, danced, played, and listened to music since time out of mind, but from 1920 onwards in the US music was effectively on tap, available day and night at the simple turn of a switch and a dial.

Music established itself as part of the common experience of daily life. It was, at once, a mundane, unremarked presence, drifting through the atmosphere, yet it also exercised a deep cultural influence everywhere. Within a decade most Americans listened to music on the radio while they were busy doing something else, at work or at home. People grew up with music, as they do today, and were immersed in music and songs from childhood to old age, associating key personal memories with particular songs and pieces of music. Mothers sang favorite songs to their babies and children, people fell in love, and out of it, with musical memories, passing through life's different phases to particular musical memories. Generations even defined themselves by the kind of music they enjoyed:

musical genres and distinctions emerged that separated one generation from another, young from old. The dead were buried to the accompaniment of their favorite music. All this seems obvious—but its ubiquity and pervasive impact was *new,* courtesy of the radio and records.

. . .

From its earliest days in the US, radio had been commercial, that is, dependent on selling products over the airways. This was quite unlike the British experience, in which the BBC was funded by taxation in the form of a license. As we have seen, US radio was substantially developed and promoted by musical entertainment, and naturally, the advertising that provided the financial foundation for radio came to use—and in some respects depend on—music for selling products and services over the airwaves. Music filled the air not only to entertain. Especially in its more mature and settled form in the 1930s, radio stations filled their programs with music not merely to entertain but also to sell and promote. In the words of Susan J. Douglas, the rise of radio market research in the 1930s saw "the start of turning you and me into a commodity—an audience—to be bought and sold, delivered to advertisers for a price."[29] Radio stations and the corporations that, in time, gobbled up smaller, local stations quickly grasped the critical importance of music in radio advertising. This was accompanied, after World War II, by television, which expanded this formula exponentially. The core philosophy survives to this day: music is basic to advertising and selling.

Today, advertising and marketing agencies regard it as axiomatic that music is central to advertising. Music in advertisements "can deliver an emotional connection with consumers and has the ability to create a relationship with the brand." The advertisers' real problem, however, is choosing the *right* music. With that in mind, commercial interests have employed scientists to explore the importance of music in people's minds, hoping that their findings might provide a key to enhancing the commercial exploitation of music and sales.[30] "Amazing Grace" came to play a role in this—and over the past fifty years it has been used as background music in advertisements to promote a multitude of products. These range from "a bakery in Minnesota and a ship in the Caribbean to a bath gel manufactured in Arizona and a llama farm in Ohio."[31] What is it about "Amazing Grace" that persuades manufactures and advertising agencies that it is an appropriate piece of music for such an array of goods and services? Why "Amazing Grace"?

. . .

By the 1930s all forms of American music were being recorded and broadcast across the US. The first hillbilly records, for instance, were pressed in 1922 and the Grand Ole Opry began to broadcast in 1925. To satisfy popular demand, a growing variety of genres of local and regional music were both absorbed into radio music broadcasts and issued on records. Country and western, hillbilly, and African American music all entered the broader national musical and commercial taste during this time, a process accelerated and diffused by the massive migrations of population during World War II, both across the US and, in the company of the US military, all over the world.[32]

Many American listeners now heard types of music they had never encountered before. This was especially true for non-Black listeners encountering the music of African Americans. Jazz, the blues, and Black singers and musicians in other genres now found a national audience via the radio. In so deeply racist and segregated a society, that expansion was dogged by inequalities and injustices, but the impact of Black music on the national culture was nonetheless massive. By the 1930s, certain bands—and their lead singers, some of them matinee idols—had emerged as national favorites. Largely via major wartime migration from the South, Chicago had become the home of major jazz musicians—a number of New Orleans's best musicians, for example, had moved to Chicago. Accessing the radio waves from there enabled Black music to become "part of mainstream American expression."[33]

. . .

The relationship between Black and white music was complex and controversial, and white musicians were sometimes accused of appropriating Black music. This mixing of American musical traditions, made possible by radio, extended beyond the most obvious blendings of Black and white music. Jazz, broadly defined, became the music of protest—and was sometimes denounced for that, as well as for a host of other, often racist, reasons. Indeed, white criticisms of Black music were underpinned by the deep-seated racism that had perpetuated the world of slavery and the oppressions of the post-slavery era for centuries. The visceral white dislike of African American music flowed from a background of entrenched US racism, manifested at its most extreme during these years by lynching, the rise of the KKK, and by the Tulsa massacre of 1921, which destroyed an entire Black community and left hundreds of African Americans dead.

This climate of American racism expressed itself in a hostility to jazz on the radio and, not surprisingly, led to censorship of the American airwaves, with bans for numerous "inappropriate" lyrics and music. Yet, despite all this, jazz filled the airwaves: "tap America anywhere in the air and nine times out of ten jazz will burst forth."[34] But to a marked degree the jazz that attained commercial, radio success was played by white bands and band leaders, adopting Black jazz music and transmuting it into something milder and more benign; music thought best suited to the newfound taste of the "broader" radio audience. Nonetheless, and thanks to radio, some African American performers became major national figures. Prominent bandleaders and singers—among them Duke Ellington, Cab Calloway, Louis Armstrong, Fats Waller, and perhaps most spectacularly Bessie Smith (who began her singing career "learning the old Dr. Watts hymns—'Amazing Grace'")—became national celebrities, at first via smaller Black radio stations, before being adopted by major stations in the cities, especially Chicago and New York.[35] Sometimes, the audiences for their music on particular radio stations were overwhelmingly white. Yet at the very same time, some radio stations refused to hire Black technical staff, while others insisted their Black employees adopt a deferential style at work. It was, of course, the years of Jim Crow. The most successful of the Black musicians were those who, like Armstrong and Ellington, were brilliant at mixing Black and white musical forms and tastes, and radio catapulted them to national—then international—stardom. "Radio took the music of African America into the heart of white America and made it our first genuine national music and one of the most important cultural exports of the century."[36]

Jazz and the blues both had their roots deep in traditional African American "spirituals, in funeral marches, and in the emotional suffering of slavery and Jim Crow." It was widely accepted that jazz offered a musical way of surviving the bitterness and woes of the world.[37] It was also a music that allowed young white people to rebel—to protest—against the styles and values of older folks. Jazz and blues seemed to express all the varied human emotions, of love and grief, of laughter and misery—that seemed inexpressible in other ways.

. . .

The end result of this welter of radio music was that music and musicians that had previously appealed to a largely local or ethnic following could now become famous, and commercially popular, from coast to coast. The potent combination of records and radio enabled singers and musicians—and the commercial interests behind them—to catch the ears of tens of millions. Not long before, popular music had depended on live performances, mainly on stage, and the adoption of songs or music by a wider public via sheet music. Now it was accessible directly in people's homes.

Music was accessible whenever someone played a record or tuned into their favorite music on the radio at home. It was also broadcast to Americans in any number of public places, in ways now familiar but that were utterly new in the 1920s and 1930s. A song, a voice, an orchestral piece could now be converted, within a matter of days, into a massive commercial success, with records selling in the tens of millions. Performers who had once been just another member of a band were suddenly pitched into stardom, their voices or instrumental virtuosity instantly recognizable—and adored—by millions. Today, it is part of the way we live, but in the interwar years, it was a totally new phenomenon. When, after 1970, "Amazing Grace" was transformed from a hymn to a global hit, it was following a pattern first established between the two world wars. Equally, it was carried along not simply by orchestral or choral ability but also by the sharp-eyed commercial interests of the entertainment industry. "Amazing Grace" was itself soon to become part of the entertainment industry. What made "Amazing Grace" a truly global phenomenon was the revolution in the technology of recorded sound and broadcasting from the late twentieth century to the present day.

· · ·

In the years after 1945, the 78 record initially held the prime position in recorded music, but the introduction of vinyl made possible the development both of the LP and the 45 by the late 1950s. It also brought about an enormous improvement in the quality of recorded sound and the ability to record music for longer periods. These changes greatly expanded the commercial market for music. This was further enhanced by the introduction of the tape cassette in the 1960s and after 1979, by the arrival of the Walkman. People could now take music with them wherever they went. These innovations were followed by the arrival of the compact disc, which not only ushered in much improved sound, but also greatly extended the length of time music could be played. By the early twenty-first century, the CD accounted for 95 percent of all music sales. But even this musical landscape was transformed yet again by the emergence of digital sound and by downloading.

The arrival of digital technology in the last years of the twentieth century "altered not only the business of music but also its creation, manufacture, and distribution."[38] As ever more people learned how to download musical files via the internet, there was a slump in the music industry. A string of legal battles about music copyright, battles of a byzantine complexity, only ended when the record companies and partners recognized the futility of their efforts to prevent the tidal wave of illicit downloading of music. Instead, they came to accept this new musical landscape and opted to work with the new technologies that were—and are—themselves changing rapidly year on year. Today, the latest of mobile phones, which are relatively inexpensive, can access millions of musical items. And thanks to a multitude of music providers (platforms), limitless music is now cheaply or even freely available on an array of personal gadgets—phones, tablets, computers, laptops, and even watches. The growth and consolidation of a range of digital platforms allowing people to access and play music have generated musical business on a stupendous scale.

A few simple facts reinforce the point, though each, of course, hides a complexity of ingredients. In 2020 the global revenue for all digital music was $1.2 billion. A year later, the digital musical revenue from downloads alone stood at $1.7 billion, while the amount generated by global streaming in that same year was $23.3 billion.[39] Sales of digital music now account for more than half of all the money earned by the US music industry. Far from suppressing the music industry, the digital age has launched an unprecedented and eye-watering boom in musical business (though the money went largely to the music corporations rather than the artists). One side issue of this astonishing shift in musical habits is that it has become more complex to assess exactly which items are popular—and how? What constitutes a hit, and how to tabulate a list of weekly or annual hits—once a simply matter of record sales or radio play—is now constructed via an intricate calculation of downloads, streaming, radio airplays, and sales.[40]

It seems likely that the rise of digital music has also changed many music lovers' attitudes to music, because many have come to accept that music can be obtained freely or at very little expense. Equally, the digital age and the development of cheap personal items of technology have transformed the ability to make, record, and distribute music. Where once the major studios held nearly all the cards, in the form of their costly studios, producers, and complex manufacturing and distributing systems, today music can be made, recorded, and distributed easily and cheaply.[41] Relatively cheap equipment now enables people to create and distribute music from their own bedrooms. They can then mix and blend their own songs with music made on the other side of the globe, before placing the final musical product in a digital location where it can be accessed and enjoyed by millions around the world. All this can be done in a matter of days. After a fashion, the music industry has, at one and the same time, become both highly domesticated and exceptionally global. As chapter 11 details, what happened to "Amazing Grace" in 2020 provides a vivid example of this process at work and adds yet another twist to the evolving story of that hymn.

The digital age utterly transformed music, the movies, and television. The introduction of iTunes—followed by other similar means of storing music—created vast and easily accessible libraries of musical choice. A seemingly endless supply of music could now be accumulated—downloaded—on a range of small personal devices. Today's digital platforms allow listeners to enjoy what is effectively unlimited access to music—for free or for a small subscription. Spotify, for example, has a library of thirty million songs. Much the same revolution changed the world of movies and television series, and today thousands of films and series are available via streaming services, notably Netflix. Thanks to the rapid spread of streaming on laptops, tablets, and smartphones, tens of millions of people now have access to a staggering range of digital entertainment, from movies to music and sports.[42]

EIGHT

"Amazing Grace" in Folk and Gospel Music

FOR ALL ITS LONGEVITY in folk and church music, "Amazing Grace" began to win new friends and supporters both between the wars and then in the years immediately after World War II. It enjoyed a new kind of popularity, notably on the back of the midcentury revival of American folk music. Though the roots of American folk music are to be found in the traditional music of immigrant and enslaved laboring people, often in remote and isolated places, American folk music was transformed after World War II. This change was bound up with the desire, among many younger Americans, to break away from the stultifying social conventions of the Eisenhower years, and from what many viewed as the stifling conformity and dictates of the state (so essential during the years of total war). All this helped to breathe new life into a musical tradition that was largely rooted in its remote rural home base. Many folk songs that had been popular at the beginning of the twentieth century were given a new lease of life in midcentury—among them "Amazing Grace." The folk music found in American workplaces had changed during the Depression and World War II, emerging "in the late 1940s as a politicized music of the American Left." But the postwar folk revival was also driven by new commercial interests. Quite suddenly, it became clear that there was money to be made from folk singing. Performers and groups who had once been happy to perform in small gatherings found that they could fill major concert halls and large public venues. In the process, folk was poised to become an important element in the musical background first of the Civil Rights movement, and later of the protests that swirled around opposition to the war in Vietnam.[1]

The most successful folk singers of the postwar years naturally owed a great deal to an earlier generation of folk singers. Pete Seeger, for example, was greatly influenced not only by his own musical family, but also by Woody Guthrie, a wandering folk singer and political activist. Guthrie—who had been "discovered" by Alan Lomax at a seminal folk concert in New York City in 1940—had led a remarkable life as a wandering laborer, hobo, and a singer of folk music. Much of his music had a political edge, and Guthrie was scornful of musical money-making. His musical range and his extensive knowledge of America's folk songs was astonishing, and it both inspired and guided Pete Seeger.[2] It was soon apparent that when suitably staged and promoted, there was a large audience for folk music in urban America. And whatever the views of the singers themselves—many folk singers were dismissive of big finance—it offered tempting commercial opportunities.

After he had spent time traveling with Guthrie, singing and agitating in various parts of the US, Pete Seeger returned to New York and worked with a number of folk groups, finally making his name with the Weavers after 1945. "Amazing Grace" (courtesy initially of Lee Hays) became part of the Weavers' regular repertoire. They sang it at Carnegie Hall in 1955.[3] Seeger, like Guthrie an unabashed communist, was by instinct and political persuasion unsympathetic to the religious nature and tone of "Amazing Grace." But by suitably changing the words, he was able to square his secular views with John Newton's message. In any case, and despite the unquestioned religious origins and appeal of "Amazing Grace," it possessed a simple, compassionate quality: an appeal to mankind at large while offering the promise of hope. Even in its original form, "Amazing Grace" was a bold assertion for humanity.

The commercial popularity of folk music—and of all other forms of music—was greatly enhanced by improved technology of recording, but especially by the introduction of LP records after 1948 and, slightly later, by the advent of TV. Whole concerts could now be broadcast and recorded live, then transferred onto both sides of a vinyl record. Sales of an LP, in a midcentury society with ever-more spare cash for consumer durables, could transform the careers of previously humble folk singers, musicians, and groups. The successful blend of a voice, a song, a concert—all carefully and cleverly promoted by an entertainment industry—could convert a folk singer into a bestselling star.

Folk music enjoyed a dizzying rise in popularity in the late 1940s and 1950s, especially among the urban young. Despite the claims, repeated time and again by musicologists—and by some folk singers—that folk was essentially a rejection of conventional, materialist life, many of its major performers became wealthy with the help of the powerful record companies that adopted and promoted their work. Organizing and recording major concerts and open-air events, pressing LPs, promoting album sales on radio and TV, and arranging tours for performers all became essential aspects of a highly lucrative entertainment industry. Like their forebears in Tin Pan Alley decades before, the music industry aimed to promote and sell musical products, whether in the form of a live concert or a record. "Amazing Grace" was to fall into the same category: a commercial item—a song—to be promoted and sold. It was a very long way from John Newton in Olney.

Though it is true that many folk singers had little to show for their efforts, those who thrived—the ones whose talents, industry, and good fortune matured into stardom—benefitted hugely from the commercialization of folk. Bob Dylan once claimed: "there was no money in folk."[4] Today he's worth an estimated $500 million. Clearly, Dylan, his music, and the world of entertainment have all been utterly transformed over the past fifty years. But the foundations of that fortune lay in his work as a folk-singing troubadour in the 1960s.

A great deal of American folk music took the form of protest against a wide range of America's faults and failings. Grievances of all kinds—labor, political, ethnic—found expression in folk music, and folk singers had long been allies of any number of US political and workers' campaigns. The Civil Rights campaigns that emerged starting in the mid-1950s were to become just the latest natural platform for musical protest, in the process generating a new range of protest songs. One of the songs recorded by folk singers in the 1950s was "Amazing Grace."

. . .

The advent of the recording industry also changed the landscape of music for Black musicians, both secular and religious. There had been an early awareness among pioneers in the embryonic American recording industry that so-called traditional music could be marketed "to immigrant groups, African-American communities, and white rural southerners." The proof lay in the production by OKeh Records of the very first record by a Black female musician—Mamie Smith, a vaudeville and cabaret singer—in February 1920. That first record sold well, and later that same year the company issued her next, *Crazy Blues*. It sold an astonishing 250,000 copies and was enormously popular in Black communities, prompting further records under OKeh's Original Race Records label.[5] It also helped to persuade other companies to issue blues and white southern vernacular music. "Amazing Grace" fitted neatly into what the recording companies of the time called "either their 'race' catalogue, or their 'hillbilly' and 'old-time' catalogs." Two years later, Brunswick Records, one of the major companies issuing recordings of the blues, was the first company to issue a record of "Amazing Grace."[6] It was part of a series of Sacred Harp singing, for which it created a special label that "incorporated shape note notation in its design."[7] This recorded version of "Amazing Grace" clearly located the song in two cultural worlds that had sustained it throughout the nineteenth century: the worlds of African American worship and of shape note choral singing.

A number of these early recordings of "Amazing Grace" were by African American "singing preachers." One of the most popular was the Reverend J. M. Gates, who described "Amazing Grace" as "one of the good old familiar hymns." Singing it, he said, "would help his listeners return to the traditional religious values of the past." The Reverend Gates also recorded a number of his powerful sermons, interspersing them with music and singing. Gates's successful recordings for Columbia inspired many other Black preachers to follow him in the years 1926–32, recording sermons and singing—and selling records in large numbers.[8] Like the Reverend John Newton almost two centuries earlier, the Reverend Gates mixed his sermons and preaching with the singing of hymns. Such records by "singing preachers" not only proved that religious music was commercially successful, but also tapped into a wide, deep stream of vernacular music and popular music-making.

The availability of recorded music and the inescapable presence of music on the radio had created a *national* audience for music that had previously been enjoyed in smaller gatherings: in churches, homes, and in small social groups in distant places in the American backcountry. "Amazing Grace," long a favorite both in Black churches and among lay folk singers in isolated places, could now be heard on the radio by an ever-expanding audience across the US.

. . .

Gospel music had long been a feature of both Black and white churches in the US. But in the interwar years, gospel music was transformed and "Amazing Grace" became a favorite gospel hymn in that process. The hymn's popularity was greatly enhanced by its presence in the repertoire of numerous gospel singers and choirs. Indeed "Amazing Grace" was to become one of the favorite performance pieces of gospel's greatest singers.

Although gospel music flourished in the twentieth century, its origins lay much further back, in the world of slavery. In the years following the Civil War, many of America's newly freed Black people worshipped much as they had under enslavement. The shouting, stomping, handclapping, and thigh slapping so loved by some participants were much disliked by those who wanted to put the musical habits of enslavement behind them. One bishop of the African Methodist Episcopal Church thought such worship "ridiculous and heathenish." Both white and African American missionary groups from the north, notably Baptists and Congregationalists, were industrious in establishing churches, schools, and seminaries in the South, and they too sought to put an end to the noisy exuberance of the camp meetings widely known as "bush meetings" because they took place in the outdoors and not in tents. This was the backdrop to the story of gospel blues in the twentieth century.

During the Second Great Awakening of the early nineteenth century, the spiritual had emerged from large camp meetings in rural areas. Gospel hymns on the other hand evolved from urban life, and many of their writers—notably Dwight L. Moody and Ira D. Sankey—drew on a wide range of musical genres when publishing their numerous editions of collected hymns. Such volumes proved highly popular in Black churches, where they joined with the musical traditions retained from the days of slavery and the love of the old Protestant hymns "by such writers as Isaac Watts, John Newton, and Charles Wesley." Some Black churches sang these hymns using the traditional method of lining out. Others used the shape note tradition of choral singing. "Amazing Grace" was among the hymns frequently sung using both systems in Black churches.[9]

At much the same time, the growing number of Pentecostal churches began to use the piano in their services, which were also characterized by a more full-bodied involvement of the congregation in the way the service was conducted. African American Pentecostal churches had spread rapidly, first across the South and then north with the waves of African American migrants heading to northern cities. In addition, from the 1890s onwards, there was a proliferation of Holiness churches, with groups often breaking away from one church to form their own. This era also saw the marked growth of city storefront churches, established in empty shops in northern city centers by migrants from the South. In all these churches, the influence of African traditions was at its strongest: "the spirit possession, holy dancing, speaking in tongues, improvisatory singing and the use of drums."[10]

A number of Baptist churches followed a similar route.[11] The gospel music that emerged from these churches, "a blend of sacred texts and blues tunes," provoked a variety of reactions. Some disliked it and thought it crude—harking back to the music of enslavement—but many more loved it and took to it with relish. Many saw it as a revival of the kind of worship that had been common before Black religious enthusiasm had been tamped down by the conventions of white worship. The sounds of what many Black worshippers considered to be "old religion" once again echoed from hundreds of African American churches across the US. In northern big-city churches, this expressive musical style was often encouraged by preachers who were keen to draw into their congregations worshippers who had migrated from the South. This was the world where gospel blues took root and flourished, ultimately developing into a major feature of African American life—and of American music.[12]

. . .

The spread of gospel music was significantly helped by the work of a number of major Black hymn-writers, notably the Reverend Charles A. Tindley, whose edited collections remained hugely popular for years. Such publications were the lifeblood of gospel music throughout the twentieth century. In 1921 for example, the publishing branch of the National Baptist Convention issued *Gospel Pearls,* a collection of "favorites of black churches in the 1920s without regard for denomination."[13] It included "Amazing Grace."[14]

Chicago was the center of Black cultural life in the North and the epicenter of gospel music. The city had been transformed by the massive migration of African Africans from the South, a transformation that met vicious white resistance at times; the Chicago race riots of 1919 left dozens dead and thousands homeless. Black communities in Chicago were served by a myriad of churches, their preachers, congregations, choirs, and soloists. That city's human links to the South nurtured the music which flowed, directly and indirectly, from southern Black churches. This was in addition to that city's swirl of musical publications. But at the heart of this story of gospel music is the life and work of one man: Thomas Andrew Dorsey. Having published his first gospel song in 1928, Dorsey went on to become the most prolific composer and

FIGURE 8. Thomas A. Dorsey, 1899–1993, the "father of gospel music." Unknown photographer, undated. Hogan Jazz Archive, Special Collections, Howard-Tilton Memorial Library, PH001268. Tulane University Special Collections, Tulane University, New Orleans.

compiler of gospel songs and to this day, his work remains hugely popular among American worshippers.[15]

Dorsey's father, the Reverend Thomas M. Dorsey, a graduate of the Atlanta Baptist College in 1894, worked as an itinerant preacher. He married a reasonably prosperous widow, Etta; their son Thomas Andrew Dorsey, born in 1899, was the first of three children, all raised in a home naturally dominated by music and religion. His mother Etta's singing left its mark on Thomas, especially the "moaning" tradition of hymn-singing that had long been a feature during slavery. Dorsey absorbed the old Protestant hymns and slave spirituals, largely via his mother's singing, but he was also influenced by the shape note singing he had learned at a rural Baptist church. Most striking of all, however, was the musical tradition of "moaning" hymns, a practice "just about known only to the black folk" according to Dorsey in later life. Such moaning was a feature of deep attachment to a hymn and was especially noticeable among people who could not read, but who were so moved by a hymn that they would rise, stamp their feet—and sing. "After a while it hits the heart, and they start to holler, hollering 'hallelujah.'" Dorsey's mother and her friends at church would "get together, get around and get to talking and then start moaning." They would moan out a hymn. Such moaning was widespread among Black congregations and became "the dominant musical source for Dorsey's gospel blues." Years later, when Dorsey explained the moaning of hymns, he used the example of "Amazing Grace."[16]

Despite this rich musical background, Dorsey failed at formal music teaching in his hometown and moved away to Atlanta, where he was attracted to the more louche musical culture in that city's bars, theaters, and brothels. The essential foundations of Dorsey's musical career were consequently shaped by blending old-time religion with the music of Atlanta's night life.[17] Bit by bit, Dorsey developed his keyboard and vocal skills, finding work in Atlanta's vaudeville theaters and absorbing the various commercial musical influences he encountered. Finally, Dorsey resolved to master the piano and immersed himself in the blues. After settling in Chicago in 1919, the year of major race riots, Dorsey soon found his stride as a session musician. Known as the "the whispering piano player," he was in great demand at parties, and played and toured with the famous blues singer Gertrude "Ma" Rainey and her Wild Cats Jazz Band, writing and arranging for the band. Ma Rainey's style and fame led to series of major successes in northern cities. It was a popular combination and Dorsey established a name for himself in the blues.[18]

In 1921, inspired by a charismatic preacher at that year's National Baptist Convention, Dorsey decided to become a gospel singer.[19] For a while he managed to keep both careers going: blues singer and pianist, and writer of religious music. At first, he sold his songs by going from church to church. Following a serious collapse in his health, between 1926 and 1928, Dorsey was unable to perform. Restored by a faith healer, the Rev. H. H. Haley—who told him, "the Lord has too much work for you to do to let you die"—Dorsey resolved henceforth to write and perform only religious music.[20] Despite the economic havoc of the Great Depression, his career flourished. In 1930, his song "If You See My Savior" was played at the National Baptist Convention in Chicago, and took the audience by storm. Along with colleagues, Dorsey founded the "world's first gospel chorus choirs" in 1931. His Dorsey's House of Music, also established that year, was the first music publisher to publish the music of Black gospel composers.

In 1932, engulfed by deep grief following the death of his wife and infant son in childbirth, he wrote "Take My Hand, Precious Lord." This hymn effectively established his name and like his earlier gospel hits, it saw Dorsey align the blues—the music he had once played commercially— to themes of hope and reassurance. "Take My Hand, Precious Lord" was later to be the Reverend Martin Luther King Jr.'s favorite hymn and was performed at his funeral in 1968.

The following year, Dorsey launched the National Convention of Gospel Choirs and Choruses. It met annually, offering workshops for gospel singers, and attracted thousands of African American Baptists from across the US. As choral director of the Pilgrim Baptist Church in Chicago (a post he held for forty years), Dorsey wrote almost one thousand songs; half of them were published. His work was the "spiritual and musical fusion of gospel hymns and blues [and] marked the emergence of the gospel song."[21] The simple message behind Dorsey's gospel blues was salvation.[22]

Dorsey's ability to improvise allowed him to switch and embellish, to change the music as he played, in church just as he had in dance halls and on stage. A brilliant pianist, Dorsey improvised as he played, creating a style that blended the blues and hymn-singing and that established itself as an essential feature of African American churches. Dorsey claimed that the blues were "really born after the slaves were free, and they were sung the way the singers felt inside."[23] He thought of the blues as expressing the way people *felt,* and despite their subsequent commercialization and popularity, never lost sight of them as a music that evolved from African American religion.

In keeping with his ability to improvise, Dorsey intended his notation of the gospel blues to serve "no other function than that of a guide, a point from which to embark upon spontaneous creativity."[24] His followers did the same, giving his music their own variations, on the keyboards and vocally. Dorsey came to exercise enormous influence within Black church and Black music, both as the sponsor of gospel blues and as the promoter of gospel choirs—and especially of female gospel soloists. He also fought with resistant churches and ministers to have his songs played and sung in their churches.

From the first, Dorsey was on the lookout for female singers. So too were theatrical agencies and record companies, who toured the South and southern churches looking for female vocal talent, signing up the most promising for recording and singing tours. Bessie Smith ("the Empress of the Blues") was already famous as a live performer, but the coming of recorded music transformed her career. In the 1920s she sold millions of records, bringing to the hymns "the earthiness and raw intensity of country blues."[25]

Dorsey searched for female vocalists in the churches that nurtured their talent. When he first heard the seventeen-year-old Mahalia Jackson in 1928 he realized at once that her voice was a perfect fit for his blend of

FIGURE 9. Mahalia Jackson, "the queen of gospel," with Thomas A. Dorsey at the piano, 1939. Unknown photographer. Hogan Jazz Archive, Special Collections, Howard-Tilton Memorial Library, OPH000777. Tulane University Special Collections, Tulane University, New Orleans.

spirituality and blues. Even as a teenager, Mahalia Jackson already had a stunning voice that could move an audience, could make them rise to their feet, clap their hands—respond. She had all the qualities and talent Dorsey was looking for. She was also a charismatic young woman, blessed with an extraordinary vocal talent. Dorsey wanted her to take a song and "to get them trills and turns and the moans and expression." He trained Jackson to smooth out her voice, encouraging her to pace her singing, to "shake at the right time, shout at the right time."[26] Gradually Jackson perfected her art: starting gently, less assertively, before moving up to a crescendo expressing the full force of her old-time religious background. It was the making of one of America's most stunning vocal performers.

Born to poor, devout Baptists in New Orleans, and related to professional performers, Mahalia Jackson adored Bessie Smith and her rendition of the blues. But like so many others, Jackson had served her musical apprenticeship in the world of hymns, particularly the hymns compiled by Watts. That hymnal had been added to and altered, year after year, becoming a standard hymnbook in churches across North America. As a child Jackson sat close to the altar along with other children listening to people "moan" the old hymns. Jackson absorbed all the musical influences of her upbringing: hymns, all-night funeral wakes, and the styles of particular singers in the congregation all blended with the street music of New Orleans to sow the seeds of her musical life.

In 1927, aged sixteen, Jackson headed to Chicago: a self-confident young woman, poised and already an accomplished vocalist. She quickly made her mark in a Baptist choir, all while making a living in domestic work, before joining three brothers and a friend to form a gospel singing group, touring local churches throughout the early 1930s. Many churchgoers disliked the way they sang. One cleric threw them out of his church: "Get that twisting and jazz out of the church."[27]

By 1936, eight years after her meeting with Dorsey, Jackson had gone solo and in 1937 she made her first record, of two hymns. Chicago boasted a number of great female gospel singers during this era, but Jackson soon stood out from the rest for her vocal strength and physical showmanship. At first, her repertoire "consisted of Baptist hymns, especially Dr. Watts' songs 'Amazing Grace' and 'The Day is Past and Gone.'"[28]

She changed the songs as she sang and moaned, moving around the venue with a vigor that enthused the audience. Banned from some churches for the way she performed, Jackson's style was adored by her fans: she "took the people back to slavery times." She reveled in Watts's hymns, but infused her hymn-singing with the blues. She "retained the folk qualities of moans, hums and holler," producing a "dramatic tension in her delivery."[29]

Foremost among Jackson's favorites was "Amazing Grace," a hymn that, like others in Watts's collection, came "out of conviction and suffering." Watt's hymns were also popular because "the worst voices can get through singing them, cause they're telling their experiences."[30] "Amazing Grace" had, in effect, "become a Negro spiritual."[31] It was the song for all those who came up "the rough side of the mountain." One verse in particular seemed to speak directly to black lives and experiences:

> Through many dangers, toils, and snares
> We have already come
> 'Twas grace that brought us safe thus far
> And grace will lead us home

Mahalia Jackson's love for "Amazing Grace" was shared by legions of African Americans and in the early twentieth century the song was ever-present in Black churches, where it naturally exercised an influence over any number of people who later became professional singers. Ira Tucker, for example, later the lead singer of the Dixie Hummingbirds, earned money as a child by going "from door to door singing 'Amazing Grace.'"[32] Gospel singers frequently described how "Amazing Grace" had figured prominently among the songs they sang as children.[33] Gospel quartets regularly included "Amazing Grace" in their performance repertoires. Baptist conventions were brought to their feet by soloists and preachers performing their own renditions of "Amazing Grace."[34] Long before "Amazing Grace" acquired its more recent global fame, it was an established fixture of African American life. In the words of the gospel singer Bessie Griffin, "Black people been singing 'Amazing Grace' for years. Nobody sings it like us."[35] And nobody sang it like Mahalia Jackson.

In the 1930s Mahalia Jackson was a major female singer in Chicago (no mean feat in a city famous for its female soloists), helping to bring a new public esteem to northern urban gospel singers. She was in great demand from all quarters, singing for politicians and at private events. Yet she was perhaps only the most famous of a number of female vocalists who transformed not only American song, but also the very nature of the way many Americans worshipped. With the rise of female gospel singers, preachers often found themselves overshadowed in their own churches. The most influential—and the best—gospel singers were women whose vocal prominence in worship represented a massive shift, a challenge to the preacher's hold over the congregation. Where else can we find such a dominant female presence in the Christian church at the time? A song, a hymn, a charismatic female voice and presence had suddenly arrived to woo and to move huge audiences as never before. Vocalists sang their favorite songs and the congregation followed them, winning over untold numbers of people to their own cherished hymns and songs. In the process, they popularized certain songs. Few had the impact of Mahalia Jackson.

. . .

Jackson's influence as a gospel singer reached far beyond gospel music's traditional boundaries. During World War II, Jackson joined Dorsey and began to perform beyond Black churches. As they traveled round the US, Jackson dazzled the crowds with her vocal magic and verve: "her glorious contralto, her fiery spirit, her flirtatious manner." Her physical presence, on stage and in the aisles, hovered between religious zeal and saucy sensuality.[36]

The twenty years following World War II have been described as "the golden age for black gospel," and Jackson became its center.[37] The 1930s had seen white gospel music dominate the airwaves, but the years after

World War II were marked by the rise of black gospel music on American radio. And there, Mahalia Jackson's was a dominant voice. By the mid-twentieth century, Jackson had become gospel's superstar. Devout and humble in person, her musical presence was a force of nature that enthralled Black and white audience alike. Though there were many other impressive gospel singers in churches up and down the US, none had the widespread American, later global, appeal of Jackson. She lived, breathed—and sang—a raw and unabashed humanity.

Jackson's 1947 recording of "Amazing Grace" is widely viewed as a classic of its kind. Though Jackson's US core base remained Black churches, where she sang with a variety of other singers, by the 1950s her fame had spread more widely, greatly helped by radio and TV coverage, initially by the famous broadcaster and journalist Studs Terkel. She had her own radio program, recorded with Duke Ellington, and sang at Carnegie Hall in 1950 to an audience of three thousand. In 1954 she made the first nationwide radio broadcast of gospel music, and two years later she appeared on the influential *Ed Sullivan Show*. She had a remarkable impact.

Jackson was now valuable commercial property, lending her name to a range of advertisements aimed at African American consumers on radio and TV. By the mid-1950s she also had a massive following among white audiences, and her name was frequently cited in major national news outlets. At the same time, her fame had spread to Europe, and her recordings for the major record companies were now accompanied by choirs and lavish orchestral backings. Columbia records promoted Jackson as the "World's Greatest Gospel Singer."

It all seemed far removed from the Baptist churches that had first sustained and nurtured her talent. Some critics, both performers and fans, disliked Jackson's lucrative turn to commercial success. Yet for all that, the nature of her singing remained much the same, and at her best, she continued to stir the crowds like no other performer. More than any other single performer, Jackson "made gospel music truly 'popular.'"[38]

By the mid-1950s, Jackson and other performers had a new and more urgent platform for their art: the growing Civil Rights movement.

Raised in the segregated South and touring throughout the US since her early adulthood, Jackson had endured the everyday racism of white Americans. In 1956, Jackson met Dr. Martin Luther King Jr. at the National Baptist Convention and agreed to travel to Alabama to sing in support of the Montgomery bus boycott. Thereafter she became a regular presence at the various Civil Rights campaigns that came to define the era. She often sang as a prelude to Dr. King's address, and sometimes used her powerful presence and fame to raise money for the cause. She also donated her own money generously. In the process, she—and others—helped to locate Black gospel music at the very heart of the Civil Rights movement. Her voice became "the soundtrack of the Civil Rights movement." Whenever Dr. King asked, Jackson came to his side and to his support: "She never refused, travelling with him to the deepest parts of the segregated south." She sang at Selma and, most memorably of all perhaps, at the spectacular March on Washington in 1963.[39] Dr. King recognized his debt to her and was fulsome in his praise for her work. Looking back on his famous 1963 Washington speech, he noted: "Millions of people all over this country have said it was my greatest hour. . . . If it was, you, more than any single person helped to make it so."[40] Jackson's most poignant performance of all was not when she sang at the inauguration of President John Kennedy in 1960, but when she sang at Dr. King's funeral in 1968.

Among all the "freedom songs" that flourished in the Civil Rights campaign—songs of protest, of resistance and affirmation—"Amazing Grace" emerged almost as a lullaby to the campaigners. Throughout 1961, the Freedom Riders riding interstate buses to challenge segregation in public transportation were arrested at the end of their journeys, in Jackson, Mississippi, and many of them were sent to Mississippi's infamous state prison, Parchman.[41] One later recalled hearing prisoners singing "Amazing Grace" at night.[42] For everyone closely involved in them, Civil Rights actions—marches, protests, sit-ins—were grueling: physically testing and always dangerous. King in particular was under intense pressure and always in danger. When at the end of a long day's march, he "found himself in a depressed state and in need of picking up, he would call Mahalia Jackson." She "would counsel, console, and sing to him. Her soothing voice and quiet ministry, even over the phone, would comfort him, especially when she sang his favourite song, 'Amazing Grace.'"[43]

Here was America's greatest gospel singer, soothing and restoring America's greatest Civil Rights leader by singing "Amazing Grace" down a telephone line. What further confirmation do we need of the importance of John Newton's simple hymn, and of how it had penetrated to the heart of American cultural life?

NINE

Music for Troubled Times

THROUGHOUT THE 1950s, deeply entrenched racism in the South continued to throw up regular acts of violence and grotesque killings that increasingly prompted anger, resistance, and political agitation. The Civil Rights movement, though bolstered by major Supreme Court decisions, was largely met by only sluggish political support from Washington, DC. But televised images of the brutal violence inflicted by white police forces and citizens on nonviolent Civil Rights protesters across the South began to shift the tide of white public opinion. African Americans had, since the days of slavery, spoken out—and sung aloud—about the racism they faced in nearly all aspects of life. Throughout, Black churches and their music had provided an unmistakable voice of protest, but starting in the mid-1950s they were joined by a growing army of new political organizations and leaders. Their aim was to press not merely against southern segregation but also for a federal guarantee of full civil rights for all African Americans. At the heart of the Civil Rights movement lay a coalition of Black churches, preachers, choirs, parishioners—and their hymns.

Not all African American churches and clerics sided with the tactics employed by the Civil Rights campaigns in the 1950s, but a coalition of churches, church leaders, powerful preachers, and singers formed a vital network for the movement. These church communities faced very real dangers: churches that sided with the movement were bombed and burned, and churchgoers, including children, were murdered by white racists. Throughout these trials, African American religion formed a bedrock for the growing Civil Rights movement. The music that was so cen-

FIGURE 10. Freedom marchers—singing—on the march from Selma to Montgomery, March 7–21, 1965. In the front, Minister James Reeb holds the hands of the Abernathy children, Donzaleigh, Ralph, and Juandalynn; behind them (left to right), Civil Rights movement cofounder Dr. Ralph David Abernathy and his wife Juanita Abernathy (behind Reeb) march beside Dr. Martin Luther King Jr. and Coretta Scott King. Unknown photographer. Abernathy Family Photographs.

tral to those churches also inspired and sustained Civil Rights activists. They sang as they rallied, as they marched, and as they camped down for the night after hard days in the streets. In 1963, marchers in Virginia had a saying: "When in doubt, pray and sing." One day, as they sang "Amazing Grace" while advancing on a line of armed police, the police line broke and let them through.[1] Hymns that had long been standard in Black churches now became the anthems for the Civil Rights services and marches. "By changing the lyrics to some old gospel tunes, they even had ready-made freedom songs."[2] Today, no one doubts the importance of that music in stiffening the resolve and emboldening the protesters for Civil Rights.

"Amazing Grace" was one of the regular items sung by Civil Rights activists, though it was only one of numerous freedom songs that came to characterize the Civil Rights campaigns. Moreover, the music that accompanied the Civil Rights movement rapidly established itself as an expression of the broader culture of American protest. It was music that derived from a great variety of musical voices and had for decades been sung and played by and about America's downtrodden and violated. The poor, the marginal, the immigrants, the freed slaves, all expressed themselves through music, and elements from each of these cultures (and more) found their way into the music that accompanied the Civil Rights protests of the 1950s and 1960s. All these strands of traditional American music came together to give musical voice to the outrage felt about the deep-seated injustices of American life. Nowhere were those injustices more blatant, more openly vicious, or more deadly than in the segregated South.

As this voice of protest grew in intensity, it attracted a number of major singers and performers, some of whom would become global stars on the wave of the protest movement. Major commercial interests, notably recording companies, helped to transform protest music into multi-million-dollar record sales—and global musical success. Who could have predicted, say in 1960, that "Amazing Grace" would, within a decade, become a worldwide bestselling record for a number of recording artists?

·   ·   ·

The racist injustices within US society had become all the more glaring after World War II, not least because that war had a powerful ideology of freedom. It was a global conflict about the freeing of subject peoples, the ending of repressive regimes, and the promotion of self-determination. How could the old European empires survive after such a conflict? And how could legally sanctioned discrimination hope to continue in the US after 1945, if only because a million Black American men and women had served in the (highly segregated) wartime military? Yet legal protection for segregation in the US did continue—at every level. But that racist ice began to crack, slowly, from 1945 onwards. The savage southern resistance to desegregation, the everyday violence inflicted on

Black Americans, and the savage killings of those who transgressed or opposed the racial order prompted new popular movements and organizations determined to bring about change, most memorably the launch of massive protests led by Dr. Martin Luther King Jr. and his supporters, Black and white. All this took place against a background of repeated and escalating outrages against protesters—beatings, imprisonments, tear-gassing, shootings, bombings, and murders. Through all this, the marches continued—and grew—and as they did so, thousands sang, most memorably "We Shall Overcome." As they marched, they were joined by stars who lent their music to the cause.

One formidable presence in the early Civil Rights campaigns in Mississippi was the indomitable Fannie Lou Hamer. A seasoned activist at all levels, and founder of the Mississippi Freedom Democratic Party, she was regularly and grossly terrorized and brutalized by southern police and racist white citizens. In 1964 she campaigned in Mississippi in the company of a young white musical prodigy, Judy Collins, who, though trained as a classical pianist, had established her name in folk clubs in a number of US cities. Collins had joined the voter registration campaign in Mississippi, crisscrossing the state with Hamer and other activists. Collins later recalled that Fannie Lou Hamer "sang 'Amazing Grace,' a song my grandmother had sung to me when I was little." More important, Collins was also struck by "the emotional impact the song had on all involved."[3] It was an experience that Judy Collins put to good use, a few years later, at the height of the Vietnam War. And her decision was to have a dramatic impact on the story of "Amazing Grace."

. . .

Protest had always been central to American folk music, but in the decade that began in the mid-1950s, folk music also became more popular than ever before. It was a period when more folk songs entered the "top ten" charts than at any other time in their history. A number of major recording stars emerged from the world of American folk music, and from the jazz and folk festivals of those years. The Civil Rights movement, especially the marches and major gatherings, provided a perfect platform for folk singers and groups, as well as for prominent gospel singers. In the process, American political protest of the era found its own musical voice, drawing on existing traditions of folk singing and Black gospel.[4] When "Amazing Grace" began to appear as a song on the Civil Rights campaigns in the 1950s, it did so because it was already familiar and widely popular in two distinct areas of American musical life: it was widespread in African American churches, and it was a regular item in the repertoire of American folk singers.

. . .

From the mid-1950s onwards, Black churches were the foundations for the nonviolent Civil Rights campaign and the drive against segregation. Black churchgoers and activists were joined, starting in roughly 1960, by college students—first Black, then also white—who staged sit-ins and civil disobedience actions. Throughout, this broadly based campaign was accompanied and sustained by protest music. Under the banner and chorus of "freedom," a wide constituency of ordinary people took to the streets. In the words of historian Eric Foner, "Together, they restored to freedom the critical edge often lost in Cold War triumphalism, making it once again the rallying cry of the dispossessed."[5] Behind the various political demands there lay a simple insistence on equality for all American citizens, the equality enshrined in the Declaration of Independence. Dr. Martin Luther King Jr. not only emerged as the movement's indefatigable and charismatic leader, but also came to personify the campaign. His memorable oratory drew on his deep understanding of the Bible and of the sacred music that had formed both his scholarly background and the musical chorus to his life. The resistance of the segregated South and the reluctance of Washington to intervene finally cracked, first with the Civil Rights Act of 1964, then in 1965 when President Johnson demanded legislation to guarantee Black voting rights. Remarkably, Johnson concluded his speech by quoting from the song that had become the battle cry of the Civil Rights movement, "We

Shall Overcome." It was an astonishing moment: the president of the United States appropriating the very language used by marchers and street demonstrators. In that very same year, the same president made the momentous decision to send combat troops to Vietnam.

Though the Civil Rights protests of the early 1960s focused on the outrages suffered by African Americans, the movement had been bolstered by small but growing numbers of young white people, especially students. In part, this was a reflection of a major shift in the demography and economy of the US. The old heavy industries, coal and steel for example, saw technological changes that drastically reduced their need for armies of laboring people. By the mid-1960s, thanks to a massive expansion of higher education, there were many more college students than coal miners or steel workers. The example of Black activists and Civil Rights campaigners in the South became a guiding inspiration for young, white protesters, drawn substantially from the new and rapidly expanding ranks of students, many of whom now took to the streets or occupied buildings. Their outrage was directed at a president who, though willing to send troops to Vietnam, to the Congo, and to the Caribbean, was reluctant to protect Black American citizens in the South. By the mid-1960s it was as if the peaceful Civil Rights campaigns of the previous decade were being transformed into a very different form of protest. What nurtured this change, and what gave American protest an edge and an often violent expression, was the Vietnam War.

Domestic politics blurred with foreign affairs to create a much changed American political atmosphere, not least because of the disproportionate numbers of Black and Hispanic men drafted to fight in Vietnam. American protest movements now brought together a new and unusual alliance, the nation's dispossessed and excluded campaigning alongside the children of America's better-off. The rising tide of opposition to the war among students was partly driven by fear of being drafted. Strife on the campuses of the nation's most prestigious institutions, marches and demonstrations by tens of thousands, urban violence that taxed civil and military authorities to the limit—all fermented a social and political brew that had a grim focus on the war in Vietnam.

That war, and the turmoil of domestic US protest against it, also developed its own musical chorus, though this time it was the raucous, angry musical background of the counterculture. Much of the music of the earlier Civil Rights campaign lived on, sung and played by performers who had become skilled at entertaining, enthusing, and rousing large crowds of protesters. Now it was overlaid by an aggressive musical anger and by the harsher tones of rock. As the war dragged on, as the casualties mounted, millions of young Americans turned against the war—and against the values of their parents.[6]

· · ·

In March 1965 President Johnson sent combat troops to Vietnam and by the end of that decade, almost half a million American troops were based in that country. The war unleashed unprecedented protest within the US. The military disasters, the horrific loss of life, the savagery of the fighting, the traumas of returning soldiers—all relayed to the wider world by on-site TV coverage—created an outraged opposition the world over, but especially in the US. The anger of those times was even audible in its music. In 1965, "the Civil Rights Movement was now a national battle, and the assassination of John F. Kennedy, and the escalation of the Vietnam War all provided much fodder for the average folk artist."[7] It reached such a crescendo of hostility that many people felt there was a desperate need for calm. Something was required to bring comfort, something to soothe rather than inflame. There was a need for some expression of healing rather than strife and violence. "Amazing Grace" fitted the bill.

· · ·

"Amazing Grace," by now an established part of America's musical culture, could be heard wherever protest or antiwar crowds gathered. Perhaps the best known and remembered of such massive gatherings was at Woodstock in upstate New York, where, at midnight on August 15, 1969, Arlo Guthrie (son of Woody) sang "Amazing Grace" to a crowd estimated at four hundred thousand people. Even with modern amplification equipment, something special was needed to draw such huge crowds into the music. The answer was both simple and tried and tested. Performers went back to the traditional "lining out" method of incorporating a crowd into a choral response. At this and subsequent major folk gatherings, when singers wanted to encourage the crowd to sing "Amazing Grace," they resorted to lining out the song. For his part, Arlo Guthrie prefaced one performance of "Amazing Grace" with his own potted history of the hymn, though it was garbled and largely incorrect. He told how John Newton, "in the middle of the ocean . . . changed his mind and turned the boat around. He took everybody back home."[8] Guthrie then proceeded to give the words to each line of "Amazing Grace" before singing it, the audience joining in as Guthrie had prompted. Other singers did much the same at other concerts. Joan Baez would read out a line from "Amazing Grace," then sing it and encourage the folk festival audience to join in.[9] Here, at the height of late twentieth-century American turmoil, in the midst of antiwar demonstrations and faced by huge, revived folk gatherings, we find famous performers adopting the same approach to communal singing used by musical instructors and preachers in the eighteenth and nineteenth centuries. This continuity provides part of the explanation for the enduring familiarity with "Amazing Grace" among Americans from one generation to another.

From the 1960s onwards, however, key commercial interests were also at work in the rise of protest music. The recording industry was dominated by major corporations that were always alert to the rapidly changing world of musical tastes. They were also forever seeking new ways of selling their products, of discovering and promoting singers, musicians, and their music, both on radio and increasingly on TV. Sometimes, and despite their finely tuned instincts, they were taken by surprise when an unexpected musical bonus came their way. A voice or a recording occasionally captured an unpredictable public mood—and the entertainment industry was happy to exploit the commercial bonanza that fell into their lap. This was the story of "Amazing Grace" after 1970.

.   .   .

Judy Collins had remained active in the protest movement after her campaigning in the South in the mid-1960s and, like many others, she continued to seek answers to the troubling times, as a member of an encounter group in her home city of New York. At one gathering, when feelings about the war in Vietnam were running high, Collins, remembering the pacifying impact of "Amazing Grace" in Mississippi a few years earlier, broke into an impromptu version of the song. The other people in the group knew the words and joined in. Everyone present—among them Collins's record producer—were struck both by the song and by Collins's beautiful rendition. A decision was made to record it, though no one involved had the slightest idea about the impact that this single recording of a hymn would have. It was, after all, a simple hymn—by then almost two hundred years old—familiar to millions of Americans. Yet this fortuitous coming together of Judy Collins and "Amazing Grace" was to have an unpredictable and far-reaching effect, changing the song into a global hit and helping to project Collins, already a major star, to global celebrity.

Collins and her producer gathered together a small group of friends and went to St. Paul's Chapel on the nearby campus of Columbia University. That beautiful church, opened in 1907, was initially Anglican but today is ecumenical and famous for its excellent acoustics. At first sight, St. Paul's presents a confusing architectural and religious mix.[10] The architect, Isaac Newton Phelps Stokes, so loved the finished building that his ashes and those of his wife were buried there. Outside it is dominated by a classical entrance embossed with large Latin inscriptions, all topped by a dome that looks like an imitation of St. Paul's in London. But inside, the yellow and white marble gives an immediate impression of a mosque in Istanbul. Yet its Anglican inspiration is everywhere. It is built in the form of a Latin cross and has stained-glass windows, pulpit, and choir and organ—all unmistakably Anglican. So too its tiled flooring and the seating arrangements. Yet the balconies that run along the sides convey the feeling of being in a Methodist chapel. What appealed to Judy Collins in 1970, however, were the acoustics of St. Paul's Chapel. They proved to be an ideal setting for her a capella version of "Amazing Grace," recorded there in 1970.

Judy Collins

Amazing Grace

I Pity The Poor Immigrant

J 27 074
(12008)

exulta   Super Stereo Sound

Distributed by WEA Musik GmbH. Made in Germany.

FIGURE 11. Judy Collins, record cover for *Amazing Grace* single, released November 1970. Courtesy of Vinyls / Alamy Stock Photo.

The intention was that her recording of "Amazing Grace" should be merely one track—the last one—on a new album, *Whales and Nightingales*. The album proved to be an unexpected hit and sold more than fifty thousand copies, but what caught the attention of disc jockeys was "Amazing Grace." At the time, DJs were inordinately influential in the music industry: they were the people who made the critical decisions about what should be played on their radio program. What they played, and what they promoted, was a major driving force in determining what the listening public heard, liked—and bought. DJs liked Judy Collins's "Amazing Grace"—and very quickly, so did their listeners. In response, her version of "Amazing Grace" was quickly released as a single, and, to the astonishment of the record company, it sold in the millions. It sold over one million copies in Britain alone.[11]

"Amazing Grace" had had an enduring popularity at the grass roots of American music. Occasionally, its popularity had taken people by surprise in the past: it seemed to exist just below the surface of general awareness, only to emerge periodically on a newfound wave of attention. In 1954, for example, when a broadcaster and record producer were searching for a theme song for a religious radio program, they hit on the idea of using an organ recital of "Amazing Grace." The radio audience so loved what they heard that Vee Jay Records issued the version in January 1955. It was an immediate hit and sold two hundred thousand copies in the first year.[12] Now, fifteen years later, Judy Collins had another unexpected hit with "Amazing Grace." It was a song possessed of an indefinable, peaceful quality and an appeal that crossed generations. Once it caught the attention of a new audience, it prompted a demand for more. People wanted to listen to it again and again.

"Amazing Grace" in 1970, however, was very different than it had been in the 1950s, not least because the US was very different, beset as it was by a painful war in Southeast Asia and by upheavals and conflict at home. "Amazing Grace" now stood out as a perfect song for troubled times.[13] And this was true not solely for the US. The song's blend of soothing music and positive words and imagery stood in sharp contrast to the uproar of contemporary protests. Judy Collins's record sold in the millions in the US. In the UK, it reentered the UK hit parade seven times in 1971–72.[14] In the process, the record elevated Collins, already a major star, into superstardom, her voice recognizable to millions the world over. Flushed with such (unexpected) success, Collins made "Amazing Grace" a signature tune that she sang at many of her concerts.

"Amazing Grace" did more than ignite Judy Collins's own global fame: it prompted a massive worldwide adoption of the hymn, by bands, choirs, solo musicians, and singers. This simple hymn, penned by an English preacher two centuries before, which had been loved and nurtured by all sorts and conditions of Americans at church and at home, had, within the space of only two years, become a hymn for humankind—at least in the Western world. A piece of music that had once belonged primarily to the pious and to folk singers now belonged to everyone—to anyone. In the US, it was to enter the pantheon of the nation's most-recorded music. In 2016, the Judy Collins version of "Amazing Grace" was chosen as one of that year's twenty-five songs that are added annually to the National Recording Registry of the Library of Congress, chosen "to showcase the range and diversity of American recorded sounds."[15] Though clearly a major achievement for Collins, we might also acknowledge the work of John Newton, a humble English preacher and former slave ship captain.

. . .

Many came to view "Amazing Grace" as a perfect antidote to the turbulence gripping American life. In the midst of a disastrous war in Southeast Asia, and with violence and political upheaval at home, here was a still, calm voice—Judy Collins's voice—to set against the grating hubbub of a troubled world. It was a song that offered many people solace in troubled times. For the entertainment industry, however, it meant something quite different: it offered irresistible commercial prospects. But "Amazing Grace" was not alone: the success of that song coincided with a number of other popular songs that conveyed a spiritual mood, some spelling out Christian messages, others, notably the Beatles, toying with Indian mysticism. The music industry had traditionally steered clear of sacred music, or even songs that had a religious tone, except of course for the specialized religious music market. But in 1970–71 it was apparent to many in the recording industry that religious music, far from being a commercial dead-end, might offer unexpected commercial rewards. To the surprise of everyone involved, the public had been moved by "Amazing Grace," and they had bought Collins's version in enormous numbers. Even more surprising perhaps, they were soon to buy other versions—*of the very same song*—and in equally large numbers.

. . .

Judy Collins's version of "Amazing Grace" had emerged from her own musical background in America's folk tradition and from the protest songs of the 1960s. Her success was quickly followed by a very different female singer, Aretha Franklin, whose musical background was the world of African American church and gospel music. Aretha Franklin had been born in Memphis: her father, the Reverend C. L. Franklin, was a preacher and Civil Rights activist who was friendly with a number of prominent Black performers and, of course, with other clerics. Aretha played the piano at her father's church, touring with him and singing as he preached. She was naturally influenced by her father's friendships with, among others, Dinah Washington, Sam Cooke, Mahalia Jackson, and the Reverend James Cleveland. In 1956, aged fourteen, she issued her first album, of hymns, but her musical career took off after her move to New York City and to a new record company (Atlantic) in 1966. There she worked with the legendary record producer Jerry Wexler, who recognized her strengths as a singer of pop music influenced by her gospel singing.

Over two nights in January 1972, Aretha Franklin recorded her first gospel album at the New Temple Missionary Baptist Church in Los Angeles, backed by the Southern California Community Choir. The choir had been founded in 1969 by the dominant figure in Black gospel music, the Reverend James Cleveland, an old friend of Franklin's father. At that session in Los Angeles, Franklin's rendition of "Amazing Grace" was among the most dazzling of her remarkable career. It was an interpretation rooted in the gospel tradition that reached back, via Mahalia Jackson and other powerful gospel singers, to the music of African American churches, with their own musical origins in the days of slavery.

Not all the critics liked Aretha Franklin's version of "Amazing Grace," but when it was released on a double album, titled *Amazing Grace,* in June 1972, it too was an enormous hit. It became the bestselling album

FIGURE 12. Aretha Franklin singing "Amazing Grace," New Temple Missionary Baptist Church, Los Angeles, January 1972. Still from *Amazing Grace,* film, 2018. © Sundial Pictures / courtesy of Everett Collection.

of Franklin's career—in excess of two million records were sold. The recording session, spread over two nights in 1972, was also filmed, and in 2018 it was released as a documentary film, under the original direction of Sydney Pollack. BBC Television broadcast the film in March 2022, exactly two centuries after John Newton wrote the hymn. "Amazing Grace" was now the focal point of a film of gospel music, performed by one of America's greatest singers in Los Angeles, directed by one of Hollywood's major film directors. The film was made available to a worldwide audience by one of the world's leading broadcasters. When watching that film, it is hard to imagine the hymn's humble origins in a quiet English village.[16]

Though this was just the latest remarkable aspect in the unfolding story of "Amazing Grace," perhaps the most unusual—and again unexpected—twist to this story emerged on the other side of the Atlantic. There, "Amazing Grace" was reincarnated by Scottish bagpipers. In the early months of 1971, the popularity of Judy Collins's version of "Amazing Grace" in Britain caught the attention of the bandmaster of an ancient British cavalry regiment. To mark the amalgamation of the Royal Scots Greys with a Welsh regiment, it was decided to make a recording of the pipes, drums, and military band of the new regiment, the Royal Scots Dragoon Guards. The recording, helped by a small regimental subsidy, included a version of "Amazing Grace," recorded almost by chance. The record producer, Peter Kerr, later to be a successful writer, said, "I had to persuade RCA [the record company] to let me do it because they didn't think it had much potential."[17] By one of those quirks of circumstance that seem to pepper the story of this hymn, this pipers' version was later played on a popular late-night BBC radio program. It prompted widespread enthusiasm among the listeners. The record company, aware of the recent commercial success of the Collins version, needed little persuasion to issue the Royal Scots Dragoon Guards' version of "Amazing Grace" as a single record, and once again, the public loved what they heard. In the words of the producer, that record turned out to be "the best-selling instrumental single of all time in Britain."[18] But in the version played by the Scottish pipers, it was the *tune* that was popular; there were no words attached.

In both the Judy Collins version and the recording by the band of the Royal Scots Dragoon Guards, the record companies had made a speculative investment. Although the people involved in producing and selling the record had felt that the record had some potential, no one—musicians, performers, or producers—imagined that they were launching a global bestseller that would become a favorite thereafter and widely used to promote a range of products and services, from movies to funerals.

The commercial successes of "Amazing Grace" in 1970–72 underlined the astonishing durability of the hymn. It clearly had a deep-seated fan base, and it was loved and appreciated by untold numbers of people. When offered in a suitably commercial format, "Amazing Grace" seemed to conjure up deep affection among millions of people, many of whom were unaware that, in origin, it was a piece of sacred music. Its haunting music and the benevolence of its main verses convey a universal humanity, a tranquility, and an optimism. In these years of stress and turmoil, many felt that it provided comfort.

FIGURE 13. "Amazing Grace" played by Scottish pipers became hugely popular after 1970. Photograph by Randy Robertson, 2007. CC BY 2.0.

"Amazing Grace" also maintained a wide appeal across a great variety of interpretations. It was music that lent itself to versions as widely different as Aretha Franklin's gospel singing, the haunting tones of Scottish pipers, and Judy Collins's a capella voice. Of course, this success was also driven by powerful commercial interests using their various strategies to promote and sell records. Equally, "Amazing Grace" became a song that could be used to sell other things. A veritable army of commercial interests picked up on the essential popularity of "Amazing Grace" as a means of promoting and selling goods and services. Each recorded version that rose in the hit parade needed the backing of major record companies to promote, press, and distribute the records. They were responding, initially, to a demand they had not predicted. Indeed, in the case of both Judy Collins and the Scottish pipers, the companies' production facilities were hard pressed to keep up with the public demand.

. . .

The Royal Scots Dragoon Guards' version of "Amazing Grace" was an astonishing hit. It was number 1 in the British hit parade for five weeks in April–May 1972, at its peak selling seventy thousand copies a day. Over the coming decades, it is thought to have sold thirteen million copies.[19] Moreover, the recurring popularity of "Amazing Grace," set off by Judy Collins, then joined by the pipers and magnified by Aretha Franklin, prompted a flurry of recordings by other artists, all alerted to the musical appeal of "Amazing Grace" and keen to join in the commercial bonanza. Rod Stewart, for example, included it on an album of 1971. The music industry had recognized that here was a song that could be used and promoted via any number of vocal, orchestral, and instrumental interpretations. The simple clarity of the music, the ease with which it could be adapted by different instruments—from the bagpipe to the guitar—and the way it suited a fine, crystal-clear vocalist ensured its rapid adoption by an ever-enterprising music industry. Though these musical versions of the same song might seem to appeal to very different audiences, all came together in confirming a widespread affection for "Amazing Grace." Each, in their own distinct fashion, brought "Amazing Grace" to millions of listeners.

In the space of only two years, "Amazing Grace" had created a massive Western fan base. For centuries, the hymn had maintained its own group of followers among churchgoers and folk singers, but after 1970 everything changed. From 1970 down to the present day, "Amazing Grace" became a favorite among tens of millions. In the process it became a peg on which powerful commercial forces could hang their various products. Yet its roots lay in the small English town of Olney in 1772.

TEN

A Song for All Seasons

WE KNOW, BECAUSE THOSE INVOLVED told us, that one inspiration behind recording and issuing the Judy Collins's version of "Amazing Grace" in 1970 was the vague hope among those involved that it might distract attention, if only for a few moments, from contemporary frictions and perhaps bring some sort of peace in place of unrest. It is impossible to assess how far it worked, if at all. After all, what effect could one song have at the higher levels of diplomacy, or among millions of angry citizens? Nonetheless, whether or not "Amazing Grace" had its desired impact, it had become a ubiquitous presence. In the years that followed the end of the Vietnam War, "Amazing Grace" was fixed in the American imagination as a soothing sound: a song Americans (and others of course) could turn to for momentary solace. The flurry of recordings of "Amazing Grace" in 1970–72, and the widespread popularity of so many disparate versions, in effect confirmed that song as a template for the usefulness of music in subsequent periods of social discontent, and even in moments of national celebration.[1] In 1993, for example, Judy Collins herself sang "Amazing Grace" at the inauguration of President Bill Clinton.[2]

During the following half century, tragedies and moments of national grief prompted calls for communal singing of "Amazing Grace" to soothe and pacify. Domestic terrorism, a disastrous space launch, and mass shootings all produced an abundance of national soul-searching and grief. One of the most chilling episodes perhaps was the bombing by an antigovernment extremist in April 1995 of an Oklahoma federal

FIGURE 14. "Amazing Grace" was played by pipers at the funeral of President Ronald Reagan, June 11, 2004. Photograph by David A Levy. Courtesy of United States Navy, 040611-N-6811L-025.

building, which killed 168 people. Though the perpetrator was quickly caught, the grief and outrage spread far beyond the bounds of Oklahoma itself. Only days after the bombing, a memorial service near the site of devastation, in the presence of President Clinton, was observed with a rendition of "Amazing Grace."

By the end of the twentieth century, this simple hymn had moved far beyond its role as a much-loved hymn. It was now a major feature in American musical culture. It was called on whenever the nation needed to mourn and reflect: people seemed to turn instinctively to John Newton's simple words for hope as well as comfort. Year after year, "Amazing Grace" was available to ease people's grief. As I was writing this book, yet another mass shooting shook the US: the murder of nineteen children and two teachers at an elementary school in Texas. A few days later, at a local "prayer event," the pastor played "Amazing Grace" on a violin. The bereaved present "collapsed in tears, their muffled wails blending with the song."[3]

"Amazing Grace" also offered a moment to pause and reflect on a life well-lived. It was prominent at the funerals of US leaders. President Reagan's funeral in June 2004 was a state event that took place over seven days, first in Washington, DC, and then in California. At the service in Washington's National Cathedral, an Irish tenor sang "Amazing Grace" (Reagan's paternal ancestors had emigrated from Ireland). A few days later, as Reagan was laid to rest in California, a bagpiper played "Amazing Grace." An Irish tenor, a Scottish piper—both performing an English hymn that had become quintessentially American. Though "Amazing Grace" was now performed in a variety of Christian services, and remained a popular hymn in Christian worship, it had also morphed into an American national song of praise and thanksgiving.

Americans had taken "Amazing Grace" to their hearts and now performed it whenever they felt in need of personal or collective peace and reflection. One striking feature of this was the way the hymn was increasingly played at funerals. On both sides of the Atlantic, if you tap into sources of information designed to provide guidance for the choice of music at funerals, "Amazing Grace" will invariably be high in the list of recommendations. One site even offers a choice from the "17 Best Versions of 'Amazing Grace.'"[4]

The BBC's favorite TV religious program, *Songs of Praise,* selected "Amazing Grace" as one of Britain's ten favorite hymns in 2019.[5] Funeral parlors and the broader commercial interests involved in bereavement and burials, for instance, insurance companies and other financial services covering funeral expenses, have also associated themselves with the song. If the bereaved are uncertain about which music they should choose, funeral directors readily guide them to "Amazing Grace" alongside a small number of other favorites.

"Amazing Grace" thus became not merely a spiritual solace but a musical dimension of powerful commercial interests, in this case the funeral business. The US funeral industry is worth an estimated 20 billion dollars a year, and music is integral to the smooth running of that business. Of course, the commercial importance of "Amazing Grace" has been a major factor in its history since its meteoric rise to commercial success after 1970. Some recording stars and corporations waxed fat on "Amazing Grace." Today, the same song helps advance the profitable interests of a different but very important commercial concern.

Another dimension to the story of "Amazing Grace" after 1970 is the popularity of the music when played by pipers. There is a plaintive quality to a piper's version—especially when performed to a filmed background of sunsets and waves. It is as if a solitary piper soothes the listeners, encouraging them to be at one with a natural, tranquil setting. Yet this version of "Amazing Grace" is relatively new. Though pipers had played the hymn for many years before, theirs was not the version that initially caught the public imagination. It was the recording of the Royal Scots Dragoon Guards in 1972 that effectively created a totally new interpretation of "Amazing Grace." That version, and variants of it, have inspired their own formidable genre that has now endured for more than half a century and today remains a defining interpretation of "Amazing Grace." But who, before the success of Judy Collins's version, could have imagined that Scottish bagpipers, and later other pipers, would develop a new way of performing "Amazing Grace"? Yet this interpretation is remarkably popular and maintains its appeal across generations and nationalities.

. . .

The end of the Vietnam War did not bring postwar harmony to the US. A deep legacy of anger and rancor survived that war, especially among those who suffered most: the bereaved, the disabled, and the traumatized. As the years passed, their grievances were both confirmed and compounded by the persistent revelations and memoirs of major political and military decision-makers. As the realities of their decisions were exposed, it became impossible to deny that more than 58,000 American lives had been needlessly lost in the pursuit of what was, from the first, recognized as a doomed venture—to say nothing of the deaths of more than 200,000 South Vietnamese soldiers, more than 1 million North Vietnamese and Viet Cong soldiers, and more than 2 million Vietnamese civilians. For all the subsequent breast-beating and public denials, for all the contrition and apologies from within America's political and military elite, it seemed to many that American leadership, from presidents down to battlefield commanders, had been extravagant with the lives of millions of people.

The various foreign and diplomatic policies pursued by the US after the Vietnam War were overshadowed by the attacks of September 11, 2001. In less than two hours on that beautiful morning, two hijacked aircraft crashed into the Twin Towers in New York City, another into the Pentagon in Washington, DC, and a fourth into a field in Pennsylvania. Almost three thousand people were killed in the initial attack and its immediate aftermath. No one who witnessed those events unfold live on TV will ever forget the scale and the horror they witnessed. It was, to borrow FDR's famous words about Pearl Harbor, a day that will live in infamy.

In the years that followed, at the myriad memorials and anniversaries of the 9/11 attacks, one piece of music—"Amazing Grace"—recurred time and again. Each anniversary was naturally marked by an appropriate memorial service, usually consisting of solemn speeches, prayers, personal testimonies, and suitable music. The most obvious and popular choice of music was one already firmly established in the American imagination for its soothing qualities. "Amazing Grace," no longer merely a popular hymn or folk song, was securely embedded as the template both for national remembrance and for personal recollection. When people gathered to commemorate 9/11 and to remember the dead, "Amazing Grace" was played and sung. It was even used to inspire British soldiers on the eve of battle in the war against Iraq.[6]

The tenth anniversary of 9/11 saw a rendition of "Amazing Grace" at Ground Zero in Manhattan. When the National September 11 Memorial and Museum was opened on the site of the attacks in New York City in 2014, it was marked by "Amazing Grace," sung by the widow of a man killed in the attack. Twenty years on from the attacks, "Amazing Grace" was again played there as the names of the dead were recited. That same year, at the Pentagon memorial, two pipers played, and a soloist sang "Amazing Grace." In addition to these numerous ceremonies at the sites of the attacks,

Americans remembered 9/11 at untold numbers of local ceremonies across the country, and around the world.[7] It had become for Americans a day of remembrance, not unlike the days on which other nations remember the end of the great conflicts of the twentieth century (November 11th in France and Britain, May 9th for World War II in Russia). On those American days of remembrance, the background music is invariably "Amazing Grace." It is often played alongside other major American songs and anthems, notably the "The Star-Spangled Banner," "America the Beautiful," and "The Battle Hymn of the Republic." The fact that "Amazing Grace" is now to be found jostling for attention alongside America's major national anthems is itself a revealing testimony to its astonishing rise to prominence and popularity. It had become both a song for all seasons and an anthem which seems to speak to national pride in the US.

. . .

By the end of the twentieth century, "Amazing Grace" had become a major international favorite: a song recognized and enjoyed by people in very different societies, though nowhere so overwhelmingly as in the US. It had a special meaning and resonance for the very people it had initially been aimed at—the devout. But it also occupied a special place in the affection of millions of Americans. Everywhere it evoked good sensations and feelings. No less important, it was available to anyone who wished to sing or record it—for free. The ancient origins of both the music and John Newton's words freed it from any question of copyright, with all the inevitable costs for performers. "Amazing Grace" thus offered a rare commercial windfall. It was a piece of hugely popular music and a collection of verses that were available, for whatever purpose, without any cost other than the usual expenses of recording and distribution. After the hits of the early 1970s had revealed the almost inexplicable commercial appeal of "Amazing Grace," there soon followed a veritable tidal wave of recordings by all sorts and conditions of musicians, orchestras, and singers. None of whom had to make copyright payments.

Recordings of "Amazing Grace" date back, as we have seen, to the early days of recorded sound in the 1920s. The indefatigable work of American folklorists, beginning in the 1930s, revealed the great variety of versions sung in the US, especially as a folk song in the South and in African American churches. But the *number* of recordings after 1970 was on a totally different scale. The majority of the recordings of "Amazing Grace" in the Library of Congress "Amazing Grace" Collection, acquired in 2004, were made after 1970, though large numbers range back to the earlier days of recorded sound. Indeed it was the astonishing presence of "Amazing Grace" in modern American cultural life that first persuaded the Library of Congress collectors to assemble recordings of "Amazing Grace." In the words of one of the collectors, "'Amazing Grace' has permeated American popular culture. One might say that it is our national dirge."[8] Their efforts now form an invaluable collection housed in the Library of Congress.[9] It includes variations of the song in the styles of big band, blues, classical, country, easy listening, electronic, folk, gospel, many types of jazz, "novelty," operative, pop, rap, rock, rhythm and blues, soul, and various ethnic or "world music." These categories, however, are fairly loose and there are, clearly, other genres of music within the collection. My own rough calculation, by no means precise or scientific, found nineteen different genres of music within the collection. Moreover, and though it includes an astonishing 3,049 versions, the collection stops in the late twentieth century. Many more recordings of "Amazing Grace" have been made since the collection was donated. The twenty-first century has witnessed not a slackening but a marked acceleration in the production of new versions of the song, as new singers, musicians, and musical styles emerge and all find themselves drawn to "Amazing Grace."

· · ·

In the spring of 2022, I spent many hours listening to the Library of Congress collection. Each version I chose prompted its own distinct reaction (though here I have to recognize the imponderable question of personal taste). At one moment I was enthralled and sometimes deeply moved (Paul Robeson), the next totally bored (Mantovani). Occasionally, an unexpected version bowled me over (Janis Joplin). Some versions were stunning (Jessye Norman for example), while others created the sensation of being in a club late at night (the Blind Boys of Alabama). By splicing together classical soloists (Jose Carreras and Placido Domingo) with a soul and pop star (Natalie Cole), one recording tried to evoke a sense of Christmas. Many, naturally, performed "Amazing Grace" in its original format, as a simple Christian hymn, often as part of a collection of devotional music. Others transported the listener into the company of traditional folk singers, playing scratchy instruments in Appalachia (the Old Harp Singers of Eastern Tennessee).

After days of listening to little else but "Amazing Grace," I was struck by a perhaps obvious fact: it is easy and simple to sing "Amazing Grace." Anyone with a clear voice that can hit a note cleanly and hold it has the mastery of "Amazing Grace." Such solo achievements, however, are often gilded by the backing of a large orchestra or choral assembly. To me, these sweeping musical backgrounds usually leave a sentimental and cloying impression far removed from the traditional simplicity of "Amazing Grace." Equally, just as "Amazing Grace" has been recorded by a large number of very different vocalists, it has been performed by a similar range of instrumentalists: pianists, organists, pipers, guitarists, trumpeters, violinists—even on steel drums. Finally, "Amazing Grace" has long since shifted from its home bases in Britain and the US and is now performed by singers and musicians in all corners of the world. We have recordings by reggae artists and steel bands in the Caribbean and by choirs in South Africa. This international reach and importance of "Amazing Grace" would be revealed most dramatically during the COVID-19 pandemic that began in 2020.

Here was a song—a hymn—that was unusually adaptable. It was, at one and the same time, a devotional hymn, a folk song sung from memory, and a piece easily adapted by all sorts of performers, from all corners of the world. "Amazing Grace" is now popular in any number of musical guises.[10]

. . .

In the last three decades of the twentieth century, "Amazing Grace" also infiltrated the broader world of contemporary cultural life via films. The universal language of music has always been indispensable in modern filmmaking. At its best, a soundtrack can lift a film from the mundane to the unforgettable. Occasionally, a film's music becomes more memorable than the film itself. No serious moviemaker can hope to succeed without a suitable soundtrack: music can make or break a film. It can illustrate the characters, advance the storyline, and provoke a range of emotions in the audience, from creating tension and anxiety to bringing calm. In brief, music plays an integral part in the development of all films—and in the way the audience reacts to what is unfolding before them. The choice of the right music and musical director is as vital a part of the filmmaking process as choosing the right script and scriptwriter, or the right actors. Filmmakers inevitably pay great attention to the choice of music and its arrangement in order to create the most appropriate mood, or, more often, changing moods.

By the late twentieth century, "Amazing Grace" had become so famous a musical item that it chose itself as an obvious accompaniment in a range of very different films. In *Coal Miner's Daughter* (1980), based on the life of the country singer Loretta Lynn, starring Sissy Spacek as Lynn, "Amazing Grace" was used, in its folk, lined-out version at a funeral. It was as close to reality as could be hoped for: a traditional folk rendition of the hymn, with communal, lined-out singing and scratchy musical accompaniment—in backwoods Kentucky.

In the movie *Silkwood* (1983), Meryl Streep plays the part of Karen Silkwood, a young nuclear plant worker who becomes an activist to expose grave wrongdoing. As Silkwood, Streep sings "Amazing Grace" over the film's otherwise silent final scene, which shows Silkwood's last moments (she was killed under suspicious circumstances in a car crash, on her way to deliver documents to a reporter). "Amazing Grace" highlights the courage and vulnerability of the heroine in this true story.

The emotional quality of "Amazing Grace" offered filmmakers a powerful tool. It was especially useful to express poignancy in times of mortal danger. In that role it appears in the war movie *Memphis*

Belle (1990), a fictionalized account of an actual American B-17 bomber and its crew in their daylight raids over Nazi Germany. Each bombing mission is a terrifying, nerve-racking ordeal that tests the young men to their physical and spiritual limits. As the ten-man crew piles into a jeep to drive to their plane—loaded with fuel, a ferocious volume of bombs, and heavy-caliber guns—they all sing "Amazing Grace." As the plane rolls out for take-off, an orchestral version takes over the music. The image is of a typical collection of young, white American men, apprehensive about what the mission will bring, turning to "Amazing Grace" for reassurance and comfort. The addition of "Amazing Grace" to the scene may have been fictional, but it captured the mood and the stark reality of the experience for thousands of young flyers faced with mortal danger.

Despite the song's obvious seriousness, and despite its relevance as a background to critical matters, "Amazing Grace" has also been adapted for more worldly and ephemeral roles by filmmakers. The soundtrack for the 1994 movie *Maverick*—a comical Western about high-stakes gambling, with all the gun-toting dangers involved—features an upbeat country-and-western style "Amazing Grace" sung by a choir of that era's biggest country music stars, including Reba McEntire, Faith Hill, Clint Black, Waylon Jennings, and Tammy Wynette.[11] It was merely a musical peg to round off the film, but even so, the fact that "Amazing Grace" was selected for use in such a fashion is further proof of the degree to which the song had permeated American popular musical culture. It had become a song for all seasons.

The 2006 film *Amazing Grace* is directly linked to the story of John Newton and the hymn. It was made and released specifically to coincide with the two hundredth anniversary of the passing of the British Act of Parliament outlawing the Atlantic slave trade in 1807. The bicentenary year witnessed a remarkable number of commemorations in Britain. Dozens of institutions, from Parliament down to small local libraries and schools, remembered the event with displays and exhibitions. The film's timing was perfect—and it ought to have made a major impact. It conveyed, however, an old-fashioned interpretation of the abolition of the slave trade, one that few serious scholars now accept. In essence, it was the story of the triumph of godly virtue over evil. Seen through the eyes of John Newton and William Wilberforce, this might seem a plausible argument. But a mere glance at the reality of abolition in 1807 reveals much more profound and intricate changes at work, among them the rise of popular politics, the changing nature of British economic self-interest, and the role of the outrage and resistance of the enslaved. If, as the film suggests, the slave trade was ended in 1807 because abolitionists persuaded Parliament that it was a godless evil, why *then?* Why not earlier, or later? The movie *Amazing Grace* offered an outdated descant on a familiar tune and, cinema flamboyance aside, it added nothing to an understanding of the real roots of abolition. It was also a cautionary reminder that many people, especially on the Christian right, continue to believe that abolition was the triumphant work of a few godly white men. John Newton had many achievements to his name—but ending the slave trade was not one of them.

But the most spectacular screen version of "Amazing Grace" was the documentary film of that name, a recording of Aretha Franklin's performance of 1972 at New Temple Missionary Baptist Church in Los Angeles, released in 2018. Here, the singer and the music were centerstage rather than being merely accompaniment to another story. The millions who saw the BBC rebroadcast of the documentary in 2022 were viewing the classic gospel interpretation of "Amazing Grace." The biographical portrayal of Aretha Franklin (played by Jennifer Hudson) in the 2021 movie *Respect* inevitably included Franklin's version of "Amazing Grace."

By the end of the twentieth century, "Amazing Grace" had moved far beyond its original role as a hymn for the devout. It had even shifted beyond its position as an American anthem. It was now an anthem for the West, tailored and performed by the broadest variety of musicians and singers. But in its transformation from a simple hymn into a global hit, it had also become clear that "Amazing Grace" could be used to promote and sell any number of products and services. Far removed, indeed utterly detached, from the devout environment that had spawned it in the eighteenth century, "Amazing Grace" had been absorbed into the world of big business.

Time and again, but especially post-1970, the story of "Amazing Grace" had revealed that it was remarkably adaptable. The pandemic of 2020 gave the story of "Amazing Grace" another remarkable twist.

ELEVEN

Pandemic

AN ANTHEM FOR HUMANKIND

THE ATTACHMENT OF THE US to "Amazing Grace" was strengthened in the aftermath of 9/11. Though it remained a hymn located at the heart of Christian worship, it had become at the same time a secular anthem that brought comfort and sometimes pleasure to millions of people with no religious convictions. It had become a strange and unusual mix of the devotional and the secular: an expression of people's deep spiritual faith and a statement of worldly aspirations. Moreover, in addition to its special position within the US, "Amazing Grace" found favor among people far afield. Though John Newton wrote it in the hopes of winning over congregations to his Christian message, it has been successful to a degree that Newton could never have imagined.

The song's global appeal has been driven in the past half century by technical revolutions in the recording and transmission of music. The ubiquity of internet connections and streaming music, allied to the cheapness of digital equipment for recording, has enabled people in the remotest of places to pick up, record, relay, and play music at will. For tens of millions of people, "Amazing Grace" has in this way become available as never before. On the back of these profound technical changes (all propelled by powerful commercial interests), "Amazing Grace" became a truly global anthem. But the arrival of the COVID-19 pandemic in 2020 elevated "Amazing Grace" to an even more popular and rarefied level as a hymn for a troubled world. In an era of global pandemic, "Amazing Grace" offered hope to millions worldwide who were confused and troubled and who found comfort in music.

As the COVID-19 virus first swept through populations, as death rates mounted, governments struggled to gain control, and medicine battled to find solutions, hundreds of millions of people were forced into locked-down isolation. Cut off from loved ones, friends—even from neighbors—people's isolation created new forms of hardship and suffering. In the US, the examples are legion of people once again turning to "Amazing Grace" in search of comfort. In Montclair, New Jersey, neighbors gathered in their gardens each evening to sing "Amazing Grace"—at a suitable distance from each other. Lori Marie Key, a nurse working in a COVID ward in Michigan, sang an impromptu version of the hymn for her fellow medical staff in the hospital; as she told reporters, "When I'm at work, I sing. . . . It gives me strength during difficult times and I believe it helps heal."[1] Caught on camera, her rendition proved so powerful and moving that she was invited to sing "Amazing Grace" ahead of President Biden's inauguration at a national COVID memorial event at the Lincoln Memorial.

During these first months of the pandemic, even places of worship had to lock their doors, forced to turn away millions of worshippers, who struggled to seek the spiritual comfort and support of their faith. One imaginative cleric in London decided that if the people could not go to church, the church must go to the people. At the very start of these lockdowns, a young, charismatic minister in London, the Reverend Pat Allerton of St. Peter's Church in Notting Hill, equipped a bicycle with loudspeakers and cycled round his city parish to broadcast his message. On March 26, 2020, he conducted his first "portable" service," cycling to the Portobello Road, normally a busy street lined with fashionable homes and antique shops, but now, like the entire sprawling metropolis, silent and deserted. He announced to the neighborhood that he was simply asking for five minutes of their time and then played Judy Collins singing "Amazing Grace," asking residents to join him in prayer. Doors and windows along the silent street were thrown open and the neighborhood quickly echoed to loud applause, shouts of approval, and requests that he should return. It was a stroke of courageous imagination—and had astonishing consequences.[2]

The Reverend Allerton had clearly struck a rich vein of approval: he had tapped into a deep yearning for a renewal of social life, for neighborliness and company, for noise and for music—and for reassurance. His efforts prompted an outburst of yearning for the simple, trivial incidents and sounds of everyday life—all of which had been totally silenced by the pandemic. An entire silent city—and much of the world at large—was in the grips of enforced isolation, with untold millions desperate to break free, if only for a moment, to hear and see reminders of an everyday life that had suddenly been torn away. In becoming a peripatetic preacher, Allerton had hit on a winning formula, bringing a few moments of pleasure and comfort to huge numbers of people who were not only isolated and separated from loved ones, but also afraid.

Allerton pedaled his bike to a string of London parishes, from the high-end neighborhoods of Chelsea and Kensington to the more downmarket Shepherds Bush. Wherever his loudspeakers broadcast his prayers and Judy Collins's voice, the reaction was the same—as Allerton confessed, "the cheering and whooping after I put down the microphone sent shivers down my spine." He also visited less noisy settings: a care home, a prison, and seven hospitals, where his message was as important for the beleaguered medical staff as for the patients. His visit to Charing Cross Hospital was recorded on a video that, inevitably, went viral and quickly attracted an astonishing five million viewings.[3] A single cleric on a bike, armed only with his prayers and hymns —among them "Amazing Grace"—had become a global figure. His was the voice of kindness and of humanity. It was also the voice of John Newton.

By any standards, Allerton's was an achievement that brought comfort and pleasure to untold numbers of people. It was also an illustration of what one person could achieve with a little imagination, a great deal of hard work, all laced with plenty of audacity. Predictably, the Reverend Allerton became an instant star for the national and international media.[4]

One person who saw the video of Allerton on the streets of London was Judy Collins, isolated, like everyone else, at her home in New York City. She, like so many others, was greatly impressed by what she saw of the Reverend Allerton's solitary work on the deserted streets of London—and by the impact of her own version of "Amazing Grace." By then, her recording of the song was fifty years old, yet it continued to move people. It still managed to bring freshness and comfort to people longing for some form of cheer and human contact. It seemed obvious that the time was right—once again—to revive "Amazing Grace." So it was that in 2020 (just as in 1970), Judy Collins decided to record "Amazing Grace." But this time in an up-to-date, global format.

In 2020 the technology of recording and releasing music was utterly different than it had been in 1970. But the message of the song was much the same: hope in times of widespread unhappiness and fear. In Judy Collins's own words: "Stay safe, help others and pray for the planet. I am sending this song out to all the doctors, nurses and patients. We will survive this with love and music and amazing grace."[5]

Judy Collins frequently told various media outlets that John Newton's message and personal story were as relevant in 2020 as they had been in 1772. Her manager and recording company (Elektra) agreed with her decision to rerecord the hymn. But this time, it would be very different. From her own dining room in Manhattan, in the spring of 2020, having seen a video of Allerton's work in London, Collins sent thirty Zoom invitations to thirty different countries, inviting choirs, singers, and musical guests to join her project of recording "Amazing Grace" as a "global choir," united by the amazing technology of the digital age. In the end, more than one thousand people joined Judy Collins, recording their piece in their own corner of the globe before beaming it to the master studio where they were assembled, edited, and shaped into a digital musical. Judy Collins saw the final version in early April (only weeks after sending out the initial invitation) and by the end of May 2020 it was released, with all proceeds donated to the World Health Organization. In the words of one commentator, "The song itself has become a symbol of hope during the coronavirus pandemic."[6]

The result was a tribute to modern digital wizardry and science: a technical masterpiece that brought together, in an eye-catching visual presentation, contributions of choirs from the US, Europe, Africa, and

India, alongside individual voices and instruments of famous performers and ordinary folk. Never had John Newton's words been given such a voice, or his message such a global audience. Once again, his message from 1772 seemed as relevant as ever. If any further proof was needed, it was here: "Amazing Grace" was now a song for humankind. In large part, that was driven forward by changes in the music industry.

· · ·

However we judge it, the history of "Amazing Grace" is remarkable. It has weathered changing musical fads and fashions over a period of more than two centuries, and today it is more popular than ever. The music we now use for "Amazing Grace"—the music that *defines* "Amazing Grace"—is relatively recent, but it too has survived and evolved over many years. At first, and like so many eighteenth-century hymns, the music sung to John Newton's words was varied and ill defined. As we have seen, today's modern version emerged from American folk traditions, as well as from the musical traditions of the Black church. That embryonic music was given a new format, and shaped into the music we know today, by the work of a generation of American evangelists in the nineteenth century. Their hymns, and the hymnbooks they compiled, and which linked John Newton's verses to the modern tune, imposed a musical uniformity and helped to widen the popularity of "Amazing Grace."

Though the stanzas of "Amazing Grace" originated in English church music in the late eighteenth century, they only blossomed fully in Christian worship in North America a century later. It was a protracted process, during which verses were sometimes dropped, changed, augmented, replaced. But the core stanzas of that hymn—the six verses written by John Newton—have survived and remain the essential foundations of the modern hymn.

The most enthusiastic voices that sang "Amazing Grace" in North America were those of African Americans. They sang—and "moaned"—"Amazing Grace" like no other people; they brought to it a gusto and relish unheard elsewhere. The music itself had a familiar resonance to early Black listeners: it reflected the familiar patterns of the call-and-response songs created in in the centuries of enslavement. This likeness made it relatively simple to absorb "Amazing Grace" (and other hymns) into a musical culture rooted in part in these work songs. Above all, though, John Newton's words *mattered*. African American churches, and the communities they represented and spoke for, turned to the words of "Amazing Grace" themselves for comfort and inspiration. Indeed, they might have seemed to have been written with the enslaved in mind. Paradoxical as it may seem, the words of a former slave trader spoke directly to the experiences of legions of the enslaved and to their free descendants, scattered across the US both during the years of bondage and afterwards.

This forces us to return to a question raised earlier. John Newton—a man steeped in the grotesque inhumanities and brutalities of Atlantic slave trading—created a powerful expression of hope and of salvation adopted by the very people he himself enslaved, transported, and sold. There is no evidence that he had the enslaved in mind when he wrote "Amazing Grace." Further, though scholars now think that Newton's epiphany—the moment of his conversion from slave trader to abolitionist—began much earlier than traditionally accepted, there is no evidence that John Newton recognized the significance of "Amazing Grace" for the Africans he had shipped across the Atlantic.

. . .

As we have seen, "Amazing Grace" took flight after 1970 as a secular anthem. Even in the US, where "Amazing Grace" has its strongest claims to be a popular *hymn,* it entered a national playlist alongside anthems with which all Americans could identify. It became a song that united Americans, especially in times of grief. This was one of the essential features behind African American affection for the hymn: it addressed its listeners and singers directly, speaking of their woes and miseries while offering solace. After 1970, tens of millions of other Americans responded to "Amazing Grace" for much the same reason. Its words offered the prospects of healing in troubled times.

John Newton had clearly hoped that "Amazing Grace," along with the many other hymns he wrote, would bring comfort. But his purpose was entirely religious—more than anything, he wanted his hymns and sermons to bring his listeners and readers to Christian salvation. His writings, vast and multifaceted, were designed to promote his Christian mission: to win over doubters, to strengthen the wavering, and to sustain the faithful. He did not write "Amazing Grace" as a secular advocate. "Amazing Grace" was not written by John Newton the abolitionist.

Despite the obvious religious origins of "Amazing Grace," many people who have been entranced by it over the past fifty years have confessed that they had no idea that it was a hymn. Though their numbers are impossible to quantify, many people like "Amazing Grace"—enjoying it as music, approving its apparent message—without recognizing its Christian origins. People have also been won over to "Amazing Grace" by the simplicity of its music. A single voice—simple and crystal-clear, or rich and full of feeling—or the unadorned sound of a solo Scottish piper, can catch not only the uplifting mood of the hymn, but also its essential peacefulness: a lone voice or a simple note, cutting through the hubbub and raucous babble of contemporary troubles.

Though it belonged to a musical tradition stretching back two centuries, after 1970 "Amazing Grace" burst into the world of mainstream US and global entertainment. A hymn from the past unexpectedly found itself driven forward on a huge wave of popularity. It also fitted perfectly the widely accepted template that demanded that a popular record be "musically simple, chorus-orientated, and about three minutes in length."[7]

The commercial success of "Amazing Grace" was also an example of the music industry's ability, revealed regularly from the 1920s onwards, to provide music for everyone. Each successive musical technology from the first phonographs of the early 1920s to the current streaming age made music ever more accessible. The digital age however saw "Amazing Grace" make a quantum leap and transformed the story once again. It was performed, recorded, and broadcast within a matter of days in 2020, as a global enterprise aimed at a global audience—all of whom were living under the threat of a worldwide pandemic. In the modern digital age, and under the shadow of a pandemic, "Amazing Grace" became an anthem for humankind. But a fundamental question—raised at various points in this book—still remains unanswered. What is it about "Amazing Grace" that lends itself to such global adoration, usage, and significance? Why does such a simple hymn appeal to so many millions? What has enabled it to be of such value, in so many different areas of modern cultural life? The astonishing resonance of "Amazing Grace" in all corners of American life was visible not only in the COVID-19 pandemic, but also, more ominously, in the violence that erupted on Capitol Hill on January 6, 2021.

TWELVE

With Amazing Grace

ON JANUARY 6, 2021, an insurrectionary mob attacked the Capitol building in Washington, DC, unleashing an orgy of violence, destruction, injury, and death that came close to a coup d'état. The consequences of that sobering and alarming incident continue to reverberate through American life. Late that afternoon, close to the western end of the Capitol, as part of the crowd surged towards the entrance, some of the mob began to sing "Amazing Grace." Or at least they sang a few lines of "Amazing Grace" before running out of words. No one present seemed to know what should follow. The singing had emerged from a crowd carrying banners, placards, and flags and sporting images of then-President Donald Trump, a lion (Trump had previously portrayed himself as a lion), the American eagle, and a citation from the Bible: Proverbs 30.30 ("A lion which is strongest among beasts, and turneth not away for any"). Other sections of the insurrectionists chanted "Hang Mike Pence!"—the vice president.

There was little sense that day of the soothing influence of "Amazing Grace"—or of that hymn being sung in a mood of thoughtful tranquility. It was being sung, and used, for very different purposes. Perhaps it was an assertion that the insurgents were on the brink of transporting a lost America back to a new life, one that had been lost, but now they could see. The savior in this case would be none other than Trump.[1] To most people, such an interpretation may seem bizarre, a grotesque usurpation of everything that "Amazing Grace" means to other Americans (and many other people too).

Yet the basic question remains: why did a mob of insurrectionists turn to America's best-loved hymn when involved in an act of unprecedented and rebellious violence that came close to toppling the democratic process? Though it is true that the mob included white Christian nationalists who hold the Constitution to be divinely inspired, and who reject Black Americans as fellow citizens, what was the significance, of "Amazing Grace" to a violent mob? Though the song came from only one small corner of the crowd, the fact that it was sung at all—that some thought it appropriate to sing "Amazing Grace"—is surely revealing. Equally revealing, no one knew the words of "Amazing Grace" beyond the first few lines. Perhaps "Amazing Grace" helped to strengthen the mob's determination, bolstering their resolve at a precarious moment, invigorating those overawed by the possible consequences of what they were doing? By appropriating one of America's national anthems, perhaps some in the mob felt that they were asserting the legitimacy of their actions. Perhaps "Amazing Grace" was being used as a smokescreen for actions far beyond the normal bounds of American political legitimacy. It was, in any case, a musical fig leaf offered as a partial cover for naked aggression, a shameless hijacking of a much-loved American song. Here was a most un-American act of violence against the democratic order, played out to the music of a favorite American hymn.

· · ·

It would be hard to imagine a sharper contrast between the events at the Capitol in January 2021 and the spiritual purpose of John Newton's hymn. Not one of the major interpretations of the hymn that had become global hits since 1970 had sought to place the hymn at the heart of violence or social turbulence. Indeed, the hymn's continuing appeal—and its success—had been the polar opposite: it had shot to global fame as an expression of personal and social tranquility. It appealed to millions of people as the antidote to unrest and upheaval. "Amazing Grace" was the music and message of peace and calm and it had become widely popular during periods of unrest. Yet it had also become an expression of American identity. It was a hymn that represented Americans of all sorts and conditions, secular and religious, much like other major American anthems. Perhaps that too was what the insurgents in January 2021 hoped for: to represent America, to speak and act for the nation at large. They literally and figuratively wrapped themselves in the flag and in other symbols of America, and a few of them tried to augment that patriotic image by singing an American anthem. That they only knew a few lines, and that their voices faded into the background prattle of a mob after the first verse, was the most telling aspect of the entire episode. They were mere impostors—violent, ill informed, and ill disposed— masquerading their low cunning behind a show of high principle. "Amazing Grace" had appeared to lend itself to people with dark intent, but it was they, not the hymn, who fell short when their ignorance of the hymn was exposed.

Many millions of other Americans however *do* know the hymn, and they turn to it on a multitude of occasions. They know it, word perfect, and they sing it, time and again, whenever the moment is right, and whenever "Amazing Grace" is called for.

Today, the words and music of "Amazing Grace" continue to exercise a gravitational pull over millions of devout Christians. For them, it expresses a simple affirmation of their faith. It is an ideal way of worshipping through song. The simple clarity of the music enables a huge range of people, from the finest of singers through to people who can hardly hold a note to sing as they worship. Singing is, after all, as old as the Christian church itself, though for long periods it was reserved for the priesthood. As we have seen, the emergence of choral worship on the back of popular hymns marked a major break from traditional worship in the Christian church. Starting in the seventeenth century, and especially from the eighteenth century onwards, hymns not only became popular because they were written in the vernacular, but they also opened up a more inclusive form of worship. Freed from the impediment of Latin, Christians could now worship by singing together in their own languages. "Amazing Grace" was, then, just one item in what became a large musical catalogue adopted by growing numbers of worshipers to pronounce their faith through song.

. . .

No group in the Western world might feel more in need of reassurance in song than the descendants of the millions of enslaved Africans cast ashore in the Americas by the brutality of chattel slavery. Understandably, it is among them that we encounter the most vocal and devoted attachment to "Amazing Grace." In the course of the nineteenth century, it was a hymn that took hold in African American churches in the South, and in the communities that sustained those churches, before spreading across the US in the wake of the Great Migration. "Amazing Grace" became so ubiquitous and so popular among African Americans that it sometimes seemed to be *their* hymn: it seemed to belong *to them*. African Americans knew the hymn better than others, they sang it more enthusiastically, and proclaimed its message as their own. Didn't the third stanza describe precisely the history of enslaved people?

> Thro' many dangers, toils, and snares
> We have already come
> 'Twas grace has brought us safe thus far
> And grace will lead us home

It is no small irony that these words were written by a man who had tortured Africans in the thumbscrews, who had loaded and transported hundreds of them like cattle, and who had disposed of them in North America like mere beasts of the fields. This hymn was not written by John Newton for the enslaved. It was written for parishioners in a small English town, for the local working people who would attend Newton's weekly service and sing his latest hymn as they worshipped. It was a very English hymn, written in a very English setting, and designed for English worshippers. In truth, at first it belonged to them if to anyone, though in time, it became a hymn for everyone.

What does "Amazing Grace" tell us about the author? Were these the words of a penitent seeking his own redemption for sins in an earlier life? Was Newton appeasing his much-stained conscience in a prayer that begged forgiveness? We know that by the time he wrote "Amazing Grace," John Newton was having private doubts about slavery and the slave trade, though he still had some way to go before he was prepared to denounce slavery in public. Even so, there is no evidence that slavery and its African victims were in his mind when he wrote "Amazing Grace," no indication that it was a hymn about or for the enslaved. Yet his words undoubtedly struck home, many years later, in the US, both in the last days of slavery and, more widely, in the days of freedom that followed. African Americans clearly found sustenance and hope in "Amazing Grace." Whatever his local, parochial intentions, John Newton had written a hymn that came to speak for the enslaved and their descendants—and they adopted it as their own.

· · ·

The appeal of "Amazing Grace" to devout Christians in general and to African American Christians in particular is beyond dispute, but how do we explain its impact among so many others? What about the armies of non-Christians—millions if we could count them—who have come to appreciate "Amazing Grace"? What makes "Amazing Grace" so special for people with no faith or spiritual beliefs, and people of other faiths?

A range of singers who have performed "Amazing Grace" in totally different settings (major concert halls, Appalachian folk gatherings, prisons, and rock concerts), when asked about the core appeal of "Amazing Grace," could not decide whether it lay in the music or the words.[2] The simplicity and charm of the music that finally settled on "Amazing Grace" is not, however, a sufficient explanation for the hymn's enduring popularity. After all, countless other hymns possess similar qualities. The durability of "Amazing Grace" may instead rest, quite simply, in John Newton's words. Those basic stanzas written in 1771–72 now resonate among millions of people.

Though "Amazing Grace" in the twentieth century became a standard item sung by a galaxy of musicians in compilations of sacred music, it has also been favored by performers of no faith whatsoever. Some of them were even hostile to religion. Having studied the stanzas, however, and recognized the humane message on offer, they decided to perform "Amazing Grace." They recognized words of hopefulness, the promise of a brighter future that could be earthly or in the hereafter. "Amazing Grace" speaks of having endured hardship and having survived, of having come through troubled times—yet it also offers the prospect of something better ahead. It is a hymn of reassurance and hope for both the devout and the nonbeliever, speaking to both of redemption and forgiveness for the past and hope for the future.

Despite its obvious Christian origins (though the word "God" appears only once—in the penultimate line of the last stanza), "Amazing Grace" conveys a humane quality that cuts across religious divides. Its words appeal to anyone in search of hope: to anyone who needs to find a sense of revived optimism in life, especially after harsh times or during misfortunes. It appeals to people in times of trouble and danger. But what brought "Amazing Grace" to the attention of so many people who did not attend a Christian church, and who must have encountered the hymn in some other fashion?

Without trying to suggest that today's universal popularity of the hymn is simply a manufactured phenomenon, a mood generated by powerful commercial interests, it would be wrong to ignore the role played by the music industry. Once "Amazing Grace" revealed its commercial potential in 1970, it was used and exploited time and again for commercial purposes. For more than fifty years "Amazing Grace," has been absorbed into a variety of important business interests, most notably perhaps in the massive business of funerals and of remembering the dead. It has been used—played, broadcast, filmed, and promoted—at countless ceremonies to mark an individual death or a major catastrophe. One version in particular, "Amazing Grace" played by a solitary piper, or a regiment of pipers, has become the hallmark of many such commemorative moments. The haunting sound of a piper provides a suitable mournful tone, perhaps even stirs a tearful sensation, and has become *the* version that is widely accepted as best suited to solemn moments of remembrance and reflection. (Not surprisingly perhaps, this has led to the widespread myth that "Amazing Grace" is a Scottish song.) "Amazing Grace" has become an anthem for the dead as much as a uniting sound for the living.

In the course of the twentieth century, "Amazing Grace" became deeply embedded in modern US culture, taking its place alongside a small number of songs and anthems that Americans view as a musical expression of their collective identity. And it was the American music industry that projected "Amazing Grace" worldwide. The spread of American popular culture around the world carried "Amazing Grace" (along with many other forms of music) to all corners of the world. Though one of the most influential and popular versions of the hymn was Scottish (or rather, played on a Scottish instrument), it was given global support via the influence of American popular culture. And no one expressed the power of "Amazing Grace" more poignantly than President Obama at Charleston in 2015.

President Obama's instinct that year was spot-on. His hunch was inspired: that if he sang "Amazing Grace" at the memorial service for the Reverend Pinckney and his murdered worshippers, it would prompt a choral response from the congregation. He was right to offer the Charleston congregation his own distinctive rendition. And he was correct to sense that an audience, gathered to respect and mourn the murdered victims, would follow his lead. Obama led—and the people followed. The uplifting presidential grace revealed in Obama's moving rendition in Charleston stood in stark contrast to what was heard in the attack on Capitol Hill.

ACKNOWLEDGMENTS

Most of the research for this book was undertaken in two libraries. Close to home, the music library of the J. B. Morrell Library at the University of York houses the important collection donated by the late Professor Wilfred Mellers. In Washington, DC, the Recorded Sound Research Center, in the Library of Congress, is home to the remarkable Chasanoff/ Elozua "Amazing Grace" Collection (of 3,049 recordings of "Amazing Grace"). I was greatly assisted working in that collection by the ever-helpful staff, especially by Bryan E. Cornell. I could not have undertaken work in the US however without the warm hospitality of old American friends. Patsy Sims, in Washington, DC, and Bill and Elizabeth Bernhardt, in New York City, all welcomed me, once more, to their homes.

I am also deeply indebted to a number of people whose advice and suggestions have proved invaluable in writing this book. For years, my agent Charles Walker, of United Agents, has been a great encouragement and support. My friend Steve Fenton provided yet another detailed and invaluable criticism of my initial draft, and, as before, the book is much the better for his wise commentary. I was initially guided to the specialist literature by the kind and detailed assistance of distant but generous colleagues who replied promptly and in great detail to the queries of a total stranger: I am happy to thank Amanda L. Eubanks Winkler of Syracuse University, and Glenda Goodman of the University of Pennsylvania. I was also greatly helped by my friend, the brilliant Shakespearean scholar Dympna Callaghan. Chris Clark, the distinguished American historian was again on hand as a friendly and supportive guide to areas of American history that were unfamiliar to me. Similarly, Alastair Minnis very kindly brought to my attention crucial aspects of "Amazing Grace" that had escaped my notice. I relied heavily for the illustrations on the excellent work of Katrina-Eve Manica. I am greatly indebted to Caroline Knapp for her meticulous and thoughtful copyediting of this book.

For the past fifty years, Jenny Walvin has patiently tolerated my endless discussions about my latest preoccupation. This time, however, they were often accompanied by my efforts to sing "Amazing Grace" whenever the mood took me. Without her, this book could never have come to fruition. Our grandchildren, Eleanor Lily Walvin and Max Walvin (aged three and six as I write), were much less understanding about the difficulties of writing a book, sometimes commandeering my desk, and even rearranging my notes to make way for jigsaws.

NOTES

INTRODUCTION

1. I explore this problem in my book *Freedom: The Overthrowing of the Slave Empires* (New York: Pegasus, 2019).

2. James Brewer Stewart, "Antislavery and Abolitionism in the United States, 1776–1870," in *The Cambridge World History of Slavery*, vol. 4, *AD 1804–AD 2016*, edited by David Eltis, Stanley L. Engerman, Seymour Drescher, and David Richardson (Cambridge: Cambridge University Press, 2017).

3. One-third of my book *The Trader, the Owner, the Slave* (London: Jonathan Cape, 2007) is devoted to John Newton.

4. I have been greatly helped by the recollections of that day by Dr. Simon Lewis of the College of Charleston and by the vivid eyewitness account by Julia Eichelberger, "Witnessing," *Glebe Street Hacks*, July 24, 2015, https:// glebestreethacks.org/2015/07/24/witnessing/. For the full text of Obama's speech, see "Remarks by the President in Eulogy for the Honorable Reverend Clementa Pinckney," White House, Office of the Press Secretary, June 26, 2015, https://obamawhitehouse.archives.gov/the-press-office/2015/06/26/remarks -president-eulogy-honorable-reverend-clementa-pinckney. Among the multitude of reports of that day's events, see Sarah L. Kaufman, "Why Obama's Singing of 'Amazing Grace' Is So Powerful," *Washington Post*, June 26, 2015; Jordyn Phelps, "The Story behind President Obama Singing 'Amazing Grace' at Charleston Funeral," *ABC News*, July 2015.

5. "Remarks by the President in Eulogy for the Honorable Reverend Clementa Pinckney."

6. Kaufman, "Why Obama's Singing of 'Amazing Grace' Is So Powerful."

7. Phelps, "The Story behind President Obama Singing."

8. David Eltis and David Richardson, *Atlas of the Atlantic Slave Trade* (New Haven, CT: Yale University Press, 2020), 18.

9. Voyage 90226, "Trans-Atlantic Slave Trade: Database," Slave Voyages, https://www.slavevoyages.org/voyage/database.

CHAPTER ONE

1. Quoted in D. Bruce Hindmarsh, *John Newton and the Evangelical Tradition* (1996; repr., Cambridge: William B. Eerdmans, 2001), 52–53.

2. Letter 2, January 13, 1763, John Newton, *An Authentic Narrative of Some Remarkable Particulars in the Life of *******, reprinted in *The Life and Spirituality of John Newton,* introduction by Bruce Hindmarsh (Vancouver, BC: Regent College, 2003), 19–20; hereafter *An Authentic Narrative.*

3. Letter 3, January 15, 1763, *An Authentic Narrative,* 22.

4. Letter 7, January 19, 1763, *An Authentic Narrative,* 50.

5. Letter 8, January 19, 1763, *An Authentic Account,* 56–61.

6. Letter 9, January 20, 1763, *An Authentic Narrative,* 63.

7. Letter to John Thornton, September 12, 1776, quoted in Chris Fenner, "Amazing Grace! (How Sweet the Sound)," Hymnology Archive, July 5, 2018, revised February 25, 2021, https://www.hymnologyarchive.com/amazing-grace.

8. P. N. L. Pytches, "The Development of Anglican Evangelicalism in London, 1736–1836," (master's thesis, Open University, 2007), 126.

9. Letter 4, January 17, 1763, *An Authentic Narrative,* 33.

10. Letter 4, January 17, 1763, *An Authentic Narrative,* 35.

11. Marcus Rediker, *The Slave Ship: A Human History* (London: John Murray, 2007), 50–53.

12. Rediker, *The Slave Ship,* 163.

13. James Walvin, *The Trader, the Owner, the Slave* (London: Jonathan Cape, 2007), 37.

14. "Charles Town: Descriptions of Eighteenth-Century Charles Town before the Revolution," Becoming American: The British Atlantic Colonies, 1690–1763, National Humanities Center Resource Toolbox, http://national humanitiescenter.org/pds/becomingamer/growth/text2/charlestownde scriptions.pdf.

15. Letter 11, January 22, 1763, *An Authentic Narrative,* 74–75.

16. Rediker, *The Slave Ship,* 164.

17. Rediker, *The Slave Ship,* 173.

18. Letter 12, January 31, 1763, *An Authentic Narrative,* 81.

19. Bernard Martin and Mark Spurrell, eds., *The Journal of a Slave Trader (John Newton), 1750–1754* (London: Epworth Press, 1962), 81–82.

20. Josiah Bull, *"But Now I See": The Life of John Newton* (1868; repr., Edinburgh: Banner of Truth Trust, 1998), 40–49.

21. John Pollock, *Newton the Liberator: A Biography* (Eastbourne, UK: Kingsway, 2000), 126–27.

22. I owe this point, and much else besides, to the remarkable research and publications of Marylynn Rouse. She kindly gave me her "Extract from the Journal of Captain Alexander Clunie from 1754 to 1758"; personal communication to author.

CHAPTER TWO

1. Josiah Bull, *"But Now I See": The Life of John Newton* (1868; repr., Edinburgh: Banner of Truth Trust, 1998), 61.

2. For details of Newton's time in Liverpool—and the wider story of Liverpool and slavery—see Daz White and Glen Huntley, "John Newton in Liverpool: From Slaver to Customs Official," *Bygone Liverpool* (blog), March 29, 2021, https://bygoneliverpool.wordpress.com/2021/03/29/goree-liverpool-part-two.

3. D. Bruce Hindmarsh, *John Newton and the English Evangelical Tradition* (1996; repr., Cambridge: William B. Eerdmans, 2001), 89–90.

4. Judith Jago, *Aspects of the Georgian Church* (London: Associated University Presses, 1997), 68.

5. Hindmarsh, *John Newton and the Evangelical Tradition,* chapter 5.

6. Hindmarsh, *John Newton and the Evangelical Tradition,* 258.

7. Hindmarsh, *John Newton and the Evangelical Tradition,* 199.

8. John A. Vickers, *A Dictionary of Methodism in Britain and Ireland* (Peterborough, UK: Epworth Press, 2000), 172–73.

9. Inge B. Milfull, *The Hymns in the Anglo-Saxon Church* (Cambridge: Cambridge University Press, 1996), 1.

10. J. R. Watson, *The English Hymn* (Oxford: Oxford University Press, 1997), 42–47.

11. Hindmarsh, *John Newton and the Evangelical Tradition,* 264.

12. Hindmarsh, *John Newton and the Evangelical Tradition,* 264–66.

13. Charles J. Doe, ed., *John Newton's Olney Hymns* (Minneapolis: Curiosmith, 2011), 13.

14. Hindmarsh, *John Newton and the Evangelical Tradition,* 268.

15. Hindmarsh, *John Newton and the Evangelical Tradition,* 271.

16. Bull, *"But Now I See,"* 179.

17. For this, and much else besides, I am greatly indebted to the research of Marylynn Rouse. See "John Newton's Diary," January 1, 1773, at the John Newton Project, https://johnnewton.org/Groups/252356/The_John_Newton /new_menus/Diaries/1773_1805/1773/Jan_73.aspx.

18. John Newton, *John Newton's Olney Hymns* (Minneapolis: Curiosmith, 2011), 13.

19. Bull, *"But Now I See,"* 234.

20. David Olusoga, *Black and British: A Forgotten History* (London: Pan Macmillan, 2016), chapter 5.

21. Walt Whitman, "I Hear America Singing," in *Leaves of Grass* (1860; repr., New York: Modern Library, 1993), 13–14.

CHAPTER THREE

1. Alan Taylor, *American Colonies: The Settling of North America* (New York: Penguin, 2002), 342.

2. Taylor, *American Colonies,* 345.

3. Richard J. Boles, *Dividing the Faith: The Rise of Segregated Churches in the Early American North* (New York: NYU Press, 2020).

4. Irving Lowens, *Music and Musicians in Early America* (New York: W. W. Norton, 1964), 8.

5. Charles Hamm, *Music in the New World* (New York: W. W. Norton, 1983), 34–35.

6. John A. Vickers, *A Dictionary of Methodism in Britain and Ireland* (Peterborough, UK: Epworth Press, 2000), 173.

7. J. R. Watson, "Music, Hymnology and the Culture of Methodism in Britain," in *The Ashgate Research Companion to World Methodism,* ed. William Gibson, Peter Forsaith, and Martin Wellings (London: Routledge, 2013), 233.

8. Vickers, *Dictionary of Methodism,* 173.

9. Hugh Amory and David D. Hall, eds., *A History of the Book in America,* vol. 1, *The Colonial Book in the Atlantic World* (Cambridge: Cambridge University Press, 2000), 259–61.

10. Taylor, *American Colonies,* 348.

11. Josiah Bull, *"But Now I See": The Life of John Newton* (1868; repr., Edinburgh: Banner of Truth Trust, 1998), 31.

12. Bull, *"But Now I See,"* 65, 71–73, 78–79, 183, 233–35.

CHAPTER FOUR

1. Judith Tick, ed., with Paul Beaudoin, assistant ed., *Music in the USA: A Documentary Companion* (Oxford: Oxford University Press, 2008), 4–9.

2. Alan Taylor, *American Colonies: The Settling of North America* (New York: Penguin, 2002), 178–79.

3. Tick, *Music in the USA*, 11–12.

4. Tick, *Music in the USA*, 22–24.

5. Tick, *Music in the USA*, 25–26.

6. Tick, *Music in the USA*, 28.

7. Tick, *Music in the USA*, 42–45.

8. "Amazing Grace," in Ian Bradley, *The Daily Telegraph Book of Hymns* (London: Continuum, 2005), 38–39.

9. "Amazing Grace," *Daily Telegraph Book of Hymns*, 38–39.

10. Christopher N. Phillips, *The Hymnal: A Reading History* (Baltimore: Johns Hopkins University Press, 2018), 120.

11. I am greatly indebted to Phillips, *The Hymnal: A Reading History*, for this section of the book.

12. Richard Crawford, *America's Musical Life: A History* (2001; repr., New York: W. W. Norton, 2005), 126–31.

13. Shape note singing was in many respects similar to the Appalachian folk music of the same era. See William Brooks, "Music in America: An Overview (Part 1)," in *The Cambridge History of American Music*, ed. David Nicholls (Cambridge: Cambridge University Press, 1998), 44–45.

14. Michael Broyles, "Immigrant, Folk, and Regional Musics in the Nineteenth Century," in *The Cambridge History of American Music*, ed. David Nicholls (Cambridge: Cambridge University Press, 1998), 154.

15. John Shepherd, David Horn, and Dave Laing, eds., *Continuum Encyclopedia of Popular Music of the World*, vol. 4, *North America* (London: Continuum, 2005), 137.

16. Michael C. Scoggins, *The Scottish-Irish Influence on Country Music in the Carolinas* (Charleston, SC: History Press, 2013), 80–82.

17. Steve Turner, *Amazing Grace: John Newton, Slavery and the World's Most Enduring Song* (Oxford: Lion, 2005), 150–55.

18. Scoggins, *The Scottish-Irish Influence*, 82.

19. Charles Hamm, *Music in the New World* (New York: W. W. Norton, 1983), 268.

20. For a discussion of the various tunes thought to have been sung to "Amazing Grace," see "Amazing Grace: The Tune," the John Newton Project,

https://www.johnnewton.org/Groups/231012/The_John_Newton/new_ menus/Amazing_Grace/tune/tune.aspx.

21. Chris Fenner, "Amazing Grace! (How Sweet the Sound)," Hymnology Archive, July 5, 2018, revised February 25, 2021, https://www.hymnologyarchive .com/amazing-grace. In addition, there were to be various changes to Newton's verses over the years, including the addition of a new verse by Harriet Beecher Stowe in *Uncle Tom's Cabin* (see chapter 6).

22. Turner, *Amazing Grace*, 156.

23. Patrick Carr, ed., *The Illustrated History of Country Music* (New York: Doubleday, 1979), 14.

24. Harry Eskew, "William Walker," Grove Music Online, January 20, 2001, https://www.oxfordmusiconline.com/grovemusic/display/10.1093 /gmo/9781561592630.001.0001/omo-9781561592630-e-0000029834.

25. Hamm, *Music in the New World*, 268.

26. Gilbert Chase, *America's Music: From the Pilgrims to the Present*, rev. 3rd ed. (Urbana: University of Illinois Press, 1992), 174–75.

27. Hamm, *Music in the New World*, 269.

28. Hamm, *Music in the New World*, 269–70.

29. Hamm, *Music in the New World*, 271.

30. Hamm, *Music in the New World*, 272.

CHAPTER FIVE

1. Philip D. Morgan, *Slave Counterpoint: Black Culture in the Eighteenth-Century Chesapeake and Lowcountry* (Chapel Hill: University of North Carolina Press, 1998), 581.

2. Olaudah Equiano, *The Interesting Narrative and Other Writings*, ed. Vincent Carretta (London: Penguin, 2018), 34.

3. *Felix Farley's Bristol Journal*, March 12, 1757, Bristol Central Library, Bristol.

4. Vincent Carretta, *Equiano, the African: Biography of a Self-Made Man* (Athens: University of Georgia Press, 2005), 136.

5. James Walvin, *An African's Life: The Life and Times of Olaudah Equiano, 1745–1797* (London: Continuum, 1998), 92–93.

6. Morgan, *Slave Counterpoint*, 581–82. For more on the banjo, see Laurent Dubois, *The Banjo: America's African Instrument* (Cambridge, MA: Belknap Press of Harvard University Press, 2016).

7. Morgan, *Slave Counterpoint*, 584–87.

8. Eileen Southern, *The Music of Black Americans: A History*, 3rd ed. (New York: W. W. Norton, 1997), 168–69.

9. Morgan, *Slave Counterpoint*, 418–19.

10. Southern, *The Music of Black Americans*, 175.

11. Southern, *The Music of Black Americans*, 175.

12. Morgan, *Slave Counterpoint*, 243–44.

13. Lawrence W. Levine, *Black Culture and Back Consciousness* (New York: Oxford University Press, 1972), 6–7.

14. Southern, *The Music of Black Americans*, 165.

15. Levine, *Black Culture and Black Consciousness*, 6–7.

16. Southern, *The Music of Black Americans*, 162.

17. Levine, *Black Culture and Black Consciousness*, 6–7.

18. Southern, *The Music of Black Americans*, 164.

19. Southern, *The Music of Black Americans*, 167.

20. Judith Tick, ed., with Paul Beaudoin, assistant ed., *Music in the USA: A Documentary Companion* (Oxford: Oxford University Press, 2008), 220.

21. Tick, *Music in the USA*, 220–21.

22. Southern, *The Music of Black Americans*, 152–53.

23. Southern, *The Music of Black Americans*, 155.

24. Southern, *The Music of Black Americans*, 178.

25. Morgan, *Slave Counterpoint*, 591.

26. Robert M. Marovich, *A City Called Heaven: Chicago and the Birth of Gospel Music* (Urbana: University of Illinois Press, 2015), 16.

27. Mechal Sobel, *The World They Made Together* (Princeton, NJ: Princeton University Press, 1987), 222.

28. John W. Blassingame, *The Slave Community* (New York: Oxford University Press, 1979), 38.

29. Tick, *Music in the Americas*, 223.

30. Louis Mazzari, "'Key to the Highway': Blues Records and the Great Migration," in "Senses of the South," ed. Géraldine Chouard and Jacques Pothier, special issue, *Transatlantica: Revue d'Études Américaines* 1 (2011), https://journals.openedition.org/transatlantica/5325.

31. Southern, *The Music of Black Americans*, chapter 7.

32. Southern, *The Music of Black Americans*, 227–31.

33. This tradition survived into recent years: BBC Television ran *The Black and White Minstrel Show* from 1958 to 1978.

34. Christopher N. Phillips, *The Hymnal: A Reading History* (Baltimore: Johns Hopkins University Press, 2018), 35.

35. Phillips, *The Hymnal*, 35.

36. Tick, *Music in the USA,* 236.

37. George E. Lankford, *Bearing Witness: Memories of Arkansas Slavery; Narratives from the 1930 WPA Collection* (Fayetteville: University of Arkansas Press, 2003), 59, 128.

38. Steve Turner, *Amazing Grace: John Newton, Slavery and the World's Most Enduring Song* (Oxford: Lion, 2005), 182–83.

39. Daniel Kingman, *American Music: A Panorama,* 2nd ed. (New York: Schirmer Books, 1990), 147.

40. Phillips, *The Hymnal,* 38.

41. Kingman, *American Music,* 141–45.

CHAPTER SIX

1. Eric Foner, *The Story of American Freedom* (New York: W. W. Norton, 1998), 55–57.

2. Eric Foner, *Give Me Liberty: An American History* (New York: W. W. Norton, 2005), 41.

3. Richard Crawford, *America's Musical Life: A History* (2001; repr., New York: W. W. Norton, 2005), 122.

4. Crawford, *America's Musical Life,* 121–22.

5. Crawford, *America's Musical Life,* 123.

6. Steve Turner, *Amazing Grace: John Newton, Slavery and the World's Most Enduring Song* (Oxford: Lion, 2005), 148.

7. Eileen Southern, *The Music of Black Americans: A History,* 3rd ed. (New York: W. W. Norton, 1997), 84–88.

8. For a more technical discussion of shape note music, see William Brooks, "Music in America: An Overview (Part 1)," in *The Cambridge History of American Music,* ed. David Nicholls (Cambridge: Cambridge University Press, 1998), 44–45.

9. Crawford, *America's Musical Life,* 129–31; Gilbert Chase, *America's Music: From the Pilgrims to the Present,* rev. 3rd ed. (Urbana: University of Illinois Press, 1992), chapter 10; Judith Tick, ed., with Paul Beaudoin, assistant ed., *Music in the USA: A Documentary Companion* (Oxford: Oxford University Press, 2008), chapter 25.

10. Southern, *The Music of Black Americans,* 84.

11. Charles Hamm, *Music in the New World* (New York: W. W. Norton, 1983), 276.

12. Crawford, *America's Musical Life,* 444–45.

13. Martyn McGeown, "The Life and Theology of D.L. Moody (with particular emphasis on his British Campaigns)," Covenant Protestant Reformed Church, https://cprc.co.uk/articles/moody/, accessed January 1, 2022.

14. *Manchester Guardian,* December 22, 1874.

15. *Manchester Guardian,* May 31, 1879.

16. Turner, *Amazing Grace,* 165–67; Crawford, *America's Musical Life,* 444–46.

17. David Kingman, *American Music: A Panorama,* 2nd ed. (New York: Schirmer Books, 1990), 148–49.

18. Turner, *Amazing Grace,* 167–68.

19. "Ira David Sankey, 1840–1908," Hymnary.org, https://hymnary.org /person/Sankey_IraDavid, accessed January 12, 2022.

20. Crawford, *America's Musical Life,* 446.

21. Michael Broyles, "Immigrant, Folk and Regional Music in the Nineteenth Century," in *The Cambridge History of American Music,* ed. David Nicholls (Cambridge: Cambridge University Press, 1998), 152–57.

22. Hamm, *Music in the New World,* 276–78.

23. James R. Goff Jr., *Close Harmony: A History of Southern Gospel* (Chapel Hill: University of North Carolina Press, 2002).

24. Roger Hahn, "White Gospel Music," *64 Parishes,* December 11, 2013, https://64parishes.org/entry/white-gospel-music.

25. Chase, *America's Music,* 181.

26. For an attempt to quantify the appearance of "Amazing Grace" in hymnals, see the graph "Appearance of This Hymn in Hymnals," in "Amazing Grace," Hymnary.org, https://hymnary.org/text/amazing_grace_how_sweet_ the_sound, accessed January 13, 2022.

27. Of the twelve slave hymns mentioned by Stowe in *Uncle Tom's Cabin,* "Amazing Grace" and another favorite camp-meeting hymn are given the most extensive attention. Deane L. Root, "The Music of *Uncle Tom's Cabin,*" 2007, available at http://utc.iath.virginia.edu/interpret/exhibits/root/root.html.

28. Turner, *Amazing Grace,* 167.

29. "E.O. Excell, 1851–1921," Hymnary.org, https://hymnary.org/person /Excell_Edwin, accessed June 21, 2022.

CHAPTER SEVEN

1. Dale Cockerell, "Nineteenth Century Popular Music," in *The Cambridge History of American Music,* ed. David Nicholls (Cambridge: Cambridge

University Press, 1998), 181; Daniel Kingman, *American Music: A Panorama,* 2nd ed. (New York: Schirmer Books, 1990), 322–25.

2. Richard Crawford, *America's Musical Life: A History* (2001; repr., New York: W. W. Norton, 2005), 234.

3. Crawford, *America's Musical Life,* 235; "The Piano," in *The New Grove Dictionary of Music and Musicians,* edited by Stanley Sadie, 676–83 (Oxford: Oxford University Press, 2001).

4. Kingman, *American Music,* 314–16.

5. Cockerell, "Nineteenth Century Popular Music," in *The Cambridge History of American Music,* 161.

6. See "Appearance of This Hymn in Hymnals, 1779–2020," in "Amazing Grace," Hymnary.org, https://hymnary.org/text/amazing_grace_how_sweet_the_sound, accessed December 23, 2021.

7. David Suisman, *Selling Sounds. The Commercial Revolution in American Music* (Cambridge, MA: Harvard University Press), 23–25.

8. Suisman, *Selling Sounds,* 29–32.

9. Cyril Ehrlich, *The Piano: A History,* rev. ed. (Oxford: Clarendon Press, 2002), 133–37.

10. Susan J. Douglas, *Inventing American Broadcasting, 1899–1922* (Baltimore: Johns Hopkins University Press, 1987), 300.

11. Suisman, *Selling Sounds,* 251–53.

12. Suisman, *Selling Sounds,* 16.

13. Steve Turner, *Amazing Grace: John Newton, Slavery and the World's Most Enduring Song* (Oxford: Lion, 2005), 197–98.

14. Patrick Carr, ed., *The Illustrated History of Country Music* (New York: Doubleday, 1979), 17.

15. Carr, *Illustrated History,* 17.

16. Carr, *Illustrated History,* 17.

17. Charles K. Wolfe, *A Good-Natured Riot: The Birth of the Grand Ole Opry* (Nashville, TN: Vanderbilt University Press, 1999), xi.

18. Turner, *Amazing Grace,* 201; Crawford, *America's Musical Life,* 617.

19. Suisman, *Selling Sounds,* 251.

20. Charles Hamm, *Music in the New World* (New York: W. W. Norton, 1983), 353.

21. Kingman, *American Music,* 338.

22. Suisman, *Selling Sounds,* 233.

23. Eric Foner, *Give Me Liberty! An American History* (New York: W. W. Norton, 2005), 773.

24. Foner, *Give Me Liberty,* chapter 20.

25. Crawford, *America's Musical Life,* 675.

26. Douglas, *Inventing American Broadcasting,* 306.

27. Douglas, *Inventing American Broadcasting,* 306–10.

28. Susan J. Douglas, *Listening In: Radio and the American Imagination* (Minneapolis: University of Minnesota Press, 2004), 83.

29. Douglas, *Listening In,* 10.

30. Luke Suggs, "The Importance of Music in Advertising and Branding," https://thegossagency.com/2017/01/31/the-importance-of-music-in-advertising-and-branding/, accessed July 3, 2022.

31. Turner, *Amazing Grace,* 231.

32. Robert Walser, "The Rock and Roll Era," in *The Cambridge History of American Music,* ed. David Nicholls (Cambridge: Cambridge University Press, 1998), 349.

33. Quoted in Douglas, *Listening In,* 90.

34. Douglas, *Listening In,* 92.

35. Anthony Heilbut, *The Gospel Sound: Good News and Bad Times* (1975; repr., New York: Limelight, 1997), 134.

36. Douglas, *Listening In,* 95.

37. Douglas, *Listening In,* 98.

38. David Baskerville and Tim Baskerville, *Music Business Handbook and Career Guide,* 9th ed. (London: Sage, 2010), 313.

39. Marie Charlotte Götting, "Digital Music: Statistics and Facts," Statista .com, January 6, 2023, https://www.statista.com/topics/1386/digital-music /#topicOverview, accessed June 3, 2022.

40. "How Are the Music Charts Calculated?" Ditto, July 31, 2018, https:// dittomusic.com/en/blog/how-are-the-music-charts-calculated/, accessed June 3, 2022.

41. Baskerville and Baskerville, *Music Business Handbook,* 322.

42. Robert J. Gordon, *The Rise and Fall of American Growth* (Princeton, NJ: Princeton University Press, 2016), 427–28, 435–39.

CHAPTER EIGHT

1. Philip V. Bohlman, "Immigrant, Folk, and Regional Musics in the Twentieth Century," in *The Cambridge History of American Music,* ed. David Nicholls (Cambridge: Cambridge University Press, 1998), 288.

2. Richard Crawford, *America's Musical Life: A History* (2001; New York: W. W. Norton, 2005), chapter 29.

3. This performance can be heard on *The Weavers at Carnegie Hall*, vol. 2, 1963.

4. Steve Turner, *Amazing Grace: John Newton, Slavery and the World's Most Enduring Song* (Oxford: Lion, 2005), 194.

5. Eileen Southern, *The Music of Black Americans: A History*, 3rd ed. (New York: W. W. Norton, 1997), 369–70.

6. Michael W. Harris, *The Rise of Gospel Blues: The Music of Thomas Andrew Dorsey in the Urban Church* (New York: Oxford University Press, 1992), 148.

7. Bryan Cornell and Todd Harvey, "Sound Recordings of 'Amazing Grace,' 1922–1942," Undated Typed Memo, Recorded Sound Reference Center, Library of Congress, Madison Building.

8. Harris, *The Rise of Gospel Blues*, 22–24.

9. Harris, *The Rise of Gospel Blues*, 153.

10. Southern, *The Music of Black Americans*, 452–56.

11. Southern, *The Music of Black Americans*, 262–63.

12. Ron Cusic, ed., *The Encyclopedia of Contemporary Christian Music: Pop, Rock, and Worship* (Santa Barbara, CA: Greenwood Press, 2010), 15–16.

13. Harris, *The Rise of Gospel Blues*, xvii–xviii.

14. Southern, *The Music of Black Americans*, 458.

15. "Amazing Grace," No. 21, *Gospel Pearls*, 1921, Hymnary.org, https://hymnary.org/hymnal/GP1921.

16. Harris, *The Rise of Gospel Blues*, xviii–xix.

17. Harris, *The Rise of Gospel Blues*, 21–23.

18. Harris, *The Rise of Gospel Blues*, chapter 4.

19. That same year, the National Baptist Convention published a hymnal, *Gospel Pearls*, which contained "Amazing Grace," a volume thought to be important for the way Baptists sang it. Cusic, *Encyclopedia of Contemporary Christian Music*, 16.

20. Harris, *The Rise of Gospel Blues*, 96.

21. Stephen A. Marini, *Sacred Song in America: Religion, Music and Public Culture* (Urbana: University of Illinois Press, 2003), 115–17.

22. Harris, *The Rise of Gospel Blues*, 238–24.

23. Harris, *The Rise of Gospel Blues*, 98.

24. Harris, *The Rise of Gospel Blues*, 99.

25. Southern, *The Music of Black Americans*, 372.

26. Harris, *The Rise of Gospel Blues*, 259.

27. Harris, *The Rise of Gospel Blues*, 257–58.

28. Anthony Heilbut, *The Gospel Sound: Good News and Bad Times* (1975; repr., New York: Limelight, 1997), 61.

29. "Mahalia Jackson, 1911–1972," in *The Grove Dictionary of American Music,* vol. 5, edited by Charles Hiroshi Garrett (New York: Oxford, 2013).

30. Heilbut, *The Gospel Sound,* 59.

31. Heilbut, *The Gospel Sound,* xxi.

32. Heilbut, *The Gospel Sound,* 37–40.

33. Heilbut, *The Gospel Sound,* 134.

34. Heilbut, *The Gospel Sound,* 62, 108.

35. Heilbut, *The Gospel Sound,* 235.

36. Heilbut, *The Gospel Sound,* 62–65.

37. Cusic, *Encyclopedia of Contemporary Christian Music,* 18.

38. W.K. McNeil, ed., *The Encyclopedia of American Gospel Music* (New York: Routledge, 2005), 199–200.

39. "Mahalia Jackson: Voice of the Civil Rights Movement," NPR, February 8, 2010.

40. "Jackson, Mahalia," Martin Luther King, Jr. Research and Education Institute, Stanford University, available at https://kinginstitute.stanford.edu/encyclopedia/jackson-mahalia.

41. The fictional prisons in two major movies—*Cool Hand Luke* and *O Brother Where Art Thou?*—were based on Parchman, a place which William Faulkner called "destination doom."

42. Robert Darden, *Nothing but Love in God's Water: Black Sacred Music from Sit-Ins to Resurrection City* (University Park: Pennsylvania State University Press, 2014), 30.

43. Richie Jean Sherrod Jackson, *The House by the Side of the Road: The Selma Civil Rights Movement* (Tuscaloosa: University of Alabama Press, 2011), 90.

CHAPTER NINE

1. "The Compass," *BBC Sounds,* June 23, 2016.

2. Peter B. Levy, *The Civil Rights Movement* (Westport, CT: Greenwood Press, 1998), 52, chapter 2.

3. Judy Collins, "On Rereleasing 'Amazing Grace,'" *Rolling Stone,* May 29, 2020; Cindy Stagoff, "Judy Collins Reinvents 'Amazing Grace' with the Help of a Global Virtual Choir," *New Jersey Arts,* July 6, 2020, www.njarts.net/judy-collins-reinvents-amazing-grace-with-the-help-of-a-global-virtual-choir.

4. Guy A. Mareo, ed., *Encyclopedia of Recorded Sound in the United States* (New York: Garland, 1993), 268–69.

5. Eric Foner, *The Story of American Freedom* (New York: W. W. Norton, 1998), 276.

6. Foner, *The Story of American Freedom,* chapter 12.

7. David Dicaire, *The Folk Music Revival, 1958–1970* (Jefferson, NC: McFarland and Company, 2011), 216.

8. Arlo Guthrie and Pete Seeger, *Precious Friend,* Warner Brothers, 1982, vinyl, in Chasanoff/Elozua "Amazing Grace" Collection, Recorded Sound Research Center, Library of Congress.

9. Joan Baez, "Amazing Grace," *Rare, Live and Classic,* disk 3, Vanguard, 1993, compact disk, in Chasanoff/Elozua "Amazing Grace" Collection, Recorded Sound Research Center, Library of Congress.

10. "History and Architecture of St. Paul's Chapel," Columbia University, pamphlet, n.d.

11. Stagoff, "Judy Collins Reinvents 'Amazing Grace'"; Steve Turner, *Amazing Grace: John Newton, Slavery and the World's Most Enduring Song* (Oxford: Lion, 2005), 224.

12. Robert M. Marovich, *A City Called Heaven: Chicago and the Birth of Gospel Music* (Urbana: University of Illinois Press, 2015), 246.

13. An actress who worked with Elvis Presley at the time of Dr. Martin Luther King Jr.'s murder claims that Presley was so moved by having watched King's televised funeral that he rose, in his private room on a Hollywood lot, and sang "Amazing Grace." "Interview with Celeste Yarnall: Live a Little, Love a Little," *Elvis Australia,* August 4, 2019, https://www.elvis.com.au/movies /celeste-yarnall.shtml.

14. *The Penguin Encyclopedia of Popular Music* (London: Penguin Books, 1990), 263.

15. "Did You Know? St. Paul's Acoustics Made American Music History," *Columbia College Today,* Summer 2017.

16. Mark Burford, "My Soul Is Satisfied," *American Music Review* 49, no. 1 (Fall 2019).

17. "History: Newspaper Reports the Amazing Success of Amazing Grace," *Piping Press,* February 26, 2020, https://pipingpress.com/2020/02/26/history-newspaper-reports-the-amazing-success-of-amazing-grace/. See also "Peter Kerr" biography on his website, https://peter-kerr.co.uk/bio.html.

18. Turner, *Amazing Grace,* 218.

19. Jonathan Brown, "A Blast from the Past," *The Independent,* November 30, 2007; "Pipes and Drums and the Military Band of the Royal Scots Dragoon Guard: Singles," Official Charts, https://www.officialcharts.com/artist/14571 /pipes-and-drums-and-the-military-band-of-the-royal-scots-dragoon-guard/, accessed July 5, 2022.

CHAPTER TEN

1. Wartime traditionally threw up favorite music to embody a national cause in any number of countries in the twentieth century.

2. David Dicaire, *The Folk Music Revival, 1958–1970* (Jefferson, NC: McFarland, 2011), 86.

3. Tish Harrison Warren, "Opinion: Uvalde Needs Our Prayers," *New York Times,* May 30, 2022.

4. Belinda McLeod, "17 Best Versions of 'Amazing Grace' of All Times," *Cake,* May 27, 2022, https://www.joincake.com/blog/amazing-grace.

5. "'Jerusalem' Revealed as the UK's Favourite Hymn on BBC *Songs of Praise* Special," BBC, September 29, 2019, https://www.bbc.co.uk/mediacentre /latestnews/2019/songs-of-praise-favourite-hymn.

6. "The Compass," *BBC Sounds,* June 23, 2016.

7. Many countries suffered losses on 9/11. More Britons were killed on 9/11 than in any other single terrorist outrage.

8. Undated letter, Allan Chasanoff and Ramon Elozua, Chasanoff/Elozua "Amazing Grace" Collection, Recorded Sound Reference Center, Library of Congress.

9. "About This Collection," Chasanoff/Elozua "Amazing Grace" Collection, Recorded Sound Reference Center, Library of Congress.

10. See commentary in Bryan Cornell and Todd Harvey, *Sound Recordings of "Amazing Grace,"* 1922–1842, Undated Typed Memo, Recorded Sound Reference Center, Library of Congress.

11. Lynn Shults, "Country Corner," *Billboard,* April 23, 1994, 26.

CHAPTER ELEVEN

1. Rachel Brodsky, "Covid Nurse Lori Marie Key Sings 'Amazing Grace,'" *The Independent,* January 20, 2021; Cindy Stagoff, "Judy Collins Reinvents 'Amazing Grace' with the Help of a Global Virtual Choir," *New Jersey Arts,* July 6, 2020, www.njarts.net/judy-collins-reinvents-amazing-grace-with-the-help -of-a-global-virtual-choir.

2. Astrid Joss, "Meet the Handsome Old Etonian Vicar Who Has Become the Hero of Notting Hill," *Tatler,* April 29, 2020.

3. Joss, "Meet the Handsome Old Etonian Vicar."

4. *The Telegraph,* "'Portable Priest' Brings Prayer to the People Despite Lockdown," YouTube, April 9, 2020, video, 3:53, https://www.youtube.com

/watch?v=OzY9Ckqsl78. See also Joss, "Meet the Handsome Old Etonian Vicar."

5. Rhino Records, "Judy Collins Amazing Grace to Be Recreated with Global Virtual Choir to Support WHO," news release, May 14, 2020, https://www.rhino.com/article/judy-collins-amazing-grace-to-be-recreated-with-global-virtual-choir-to-support-who.

6. Rose Pentreath, "The World Has Come Together to Sing 'Amazing Grace' and It's the Most Moving Thing," *Classic FM,* May 29, 2020, https://www.classicfm.com/discover-music/world-together-sings-amazing-grace-global-choir/; Stagoff, "Judy Collins Reinvents 'Amazing Grace.'"

7. David Suisman, *Selling Sounds: The Commercial Revolution in American Music* (Cambridge, MA: Harvard University Press, 2009), 277.

CHAPTER TWELVE

1. See Theodore Louis Trost, "The Lion, the Crowd, and Amazing Grace," *Uncivil Religion: January 6, 2021,* version 22, updated January 1, 2022, https://uncivilreligion.org/home/the-lion-the-crowd-and-amazing-grace.

2. *Amazing Grace: With Bill Moyers,* aired September 12, 1990, PBS WNET; DVD, 2012.

SOURCES AND FURTHER READING

Anyone interested in the story of "Amazing Grace" should start, as I did, with Steve Turner's important study, *Amazing Grace: John Newton, Slavery and the World's Most Enduring Song* (Oxford: Lion, 2005). We inevitably cover much the same territory, but I write as a historian, Turner as a music critic.

WEBSITES

Websites make available an astonishing volume of detail and information about John Newton, "Amazing Grace," and the world of hymnology. The following are among the most useful:

For details about John Newton's life and writing, see the exhaustive work of Marylynn Rouse in the John Newton Project, www.johnnewton.org.

Two websites are especially useful for details about hymns and the writers of hymns: Hymnology Archive, www.hymnologyarchive.com; and Hymnary .org.

The story of the Atlantic slave trade is best approached via the pioneering findings of David Eltis and David Richardson in the Trans-Atlantic Slave Trade Database, SlaveVoyages.org.

There are 3,049 recordings of "Amazing Grace" available in the Chasanoff /Elozua "Amazing Grace" Collection, in the Recorded Sound Reference Center, Library of Congress, Washington, DC. The history of this collection is explained in "About This Collection," https://www.loc.gov/collections /amazing-grace/about-this-collection.

Specialists in the field need no instruction about where to look for further information. What follows is a guide to easily accessible sources for a general reader, grouped according to the major themes covered in this book.

John Newton, Slavery, and Slave Ships

Eltis, David, and David Richardson. *Atlas of the Atlantic Slave Trade.* New Haven, CT: Yale University Press, 2015.

Martin, Bernard, and Mark Spurrell, eds. *The Journal of a Slave Trader (John Newton), 1750–1754.* London: Epworth Press, 1962.

Newton, John. *An Authentic Narrative of Some Remarkable Particulars in the Life of* ******. Reprinted in *The Life and Spirituality of John Newton,* introduction by Bruce Hindmarsh. Vancouver, BC: Regent College, 2003.

Rediker, Marcus. *The Slave Ship: A Human History.* London: John Murray, 2007.

Walvin, James. *The Trader, the Owner, the Slave.* London: Jonathan Cape, 2007.

"Amazing Grace," the Hymn

Bull, Josiah. *"But Now I See": The Life of John Newton.* 1868. Reprint, Edinburgh: Banner of Truth Trust, 1998.

Hindmarsh, D. Bruce. *John Newton and the Evangelical Tradition.* 1996. Reprint, Cambridge: William B. Eerdmans, 2001.

Newton, John. *John Newton's Olney Hymns.* Minneapolis: Curiosmith, 2011.

Phillips, Christopher N. *The Hymnal: A Reading History.* Baltimore: Johns Hopkins University Press, 2018.

Watson, J. R. *The English Hymn.* Oxford: Oxford University Press, 1999.

Music and the Americas

Chase, Gilbert. *America's Music: From the Pilgrims to the Present.* Revised 3rd ed. Urbana: University of Illinois Press, 1992.

Crawford, Richard. *America's Musical Life: A History.* 2001. Reprint, New York: W. W. Norton, 2005.

Hamm, Charles. *Music in the New World.* New York: W. W. Norton, 1983.

Kingman, Daniel. *American Music: A Panorama*. 2nd ed. New York: Schirmer Books, 1990.

Lowens, Irving. *Music and Musicians in Early America*. New York: W. W. Norton, 1964.

Nicholls, David, ed. *The Cambridge History of American Music*. Cambridge: Cambridge University Press, 1998.

Taylor, Alan. *American Colonies: The Settling of North America*. New York: Penguin, 2002.

Tick, Judith, ed. *Music in the USA: A Documentary Companion*. With assistant editor Paul Beaudoin. Oxford: Oxford University Press, 2008.

Music in Slavery and Freedom

Blassingame, John W. *The Slave Community*. New York: Oxford University Press, 1979.

Dubois, Laurent. *The Banjo: America's African Instrument*. Cambridge, MA: Belknap Press of Harvard University Press, 2016.

Levine, Lawrence W. *Black Culture and Black Consciousness*. New York: Oxford University Press, 1977.

Morgan, Philip D. *Slave Counterpoint: Black Culture in the Eighteenth-Century Chesapeake and Lowcountry*. Chapel Hill: University of North Carolina Press, 1998.

Southern, Eileen. *The Music of Black Americans: A History*. 3rd ed. New York: W. W. Norton, 1997.

The Blues, Gospel, and Churches

Goff, James R., Jr. *Close Harmony: A History of Southern Gospel*. Chapel Hill: University of North Carolina Press, 2002.

Harris, Michael W. *The Rise of Gospel Blues: The Music of Thomas Andrew Dorsey in the Urban Church*. New York: Oxford University Press, 1992.

Heilbut, Anthony. *The Gospel Sound: Good News and Bad Times*. 1975. Reprint, New York: Limelight, 1997.

Jackson, George Pullen. *Spiritual Folk-Songs of Early America*. New York: Dover, 1964.

Lomax, John A., and Alan Lomax. *Our Singing Country: Folk Songs and Ballads*. Mineola, NY: Dover, 2000.

Marini, Stephen A. *Sacred Song in America: Religion, Music and Public Culture*. Urbana: University of Illinois Press, 2003.

The Twentieth Century

Barlow, William. *Voice Over: The Making of Black Radio*. Philadelphia: Temple University Press, 1999.

Cusic, Ron, ed. *The Encyclopedia of Contemporary Christian Music: Pop, Rock, and Worship*. Santa Barbara, CA: Greenwood Press, 2010.

Douglas, Susan J. *Inventing American Broadcasting, 1899–1922*. Baltimore: Johns Hopkins University Press, 1987.

———. *Listening In: Radio and the American Imagination*. Minneapolis: University of Minnesota Press, 2004.

Foner, Eric. *The Story of American Freedom*. New York: W. W. Norton, 1998.

Hilmes, Michele. *Radio Voices: American Broadcasting, 1922–1932*. Minneapolis: University of Minnesota Press, 1997.

Levy, Peter B. *The Civil Rights Movement*. Westport, CT: Greenwood Press, 1998.

———, ed. *Let Freedom Ring: A Documentary History of the Modern Civil Rights Movement*. Westport, CT: Greenwood Press, 1992.

Mareo, Guy A., ed. *Encyclopedia of Recorded Sound in the United States*. New York: Garland, 1993.

Suisman, David. *Selling Sounds: The Commercial Revolution in American Music*. Cambridge, MA: Harvard University Press, 2009.

INDEX

culture; "Amazing Grace"; folk music and singing; hymns and hymn singing; music *entries*
anti–Vietnam War protests and protest music, 105, 127–29; Judy Collins and "Amazing Grace," 125, 130–34, 131*fig.*, 137–38, 152–54, 157–58
Appalachian music, 51–52, 86, 98, 173n13
Argyle (ship), 19–20
Armstrong, Louis, 99, 100
Army Hymn-Book, The, 48
Atlantic Records, 134

Baez, Joan, 129
Baptist churches and worship, 68, 71, 74, 108–9, 109–10. *See also* gospel music
Bay Psalm Book, The, 44
Black Crowes, 52
Black culture and communities. *See* African American *entries*; enslaved people
Bliss, Philip, 80, 81
blues, 98, 100, 107, 109–10, 112; Dorsey's blues-gospel fusion, 112–15. *See also* gospel music
blues singers: Bessie Smith, 99, 114; Mahalia Jackson, 114–21, 115*fig.*; "Ma" Rainey, 113
Britain: abolitionism and abolition in, 9, 34–35, 148–49; "Amazing Grace" in, 35, 36, 46–47, 53, 132, 135–37, 141, 143; American evangelists in, 78–80. *See also* Church of England; *specific cities and towns*
Broadman Hymnal (McKinney), 81
Brownlow (ship), 7–8, 16–18, 19
Brunswick Records, 107

call-and-response singing, 6, 31, 59–60, 72
camp meetings and revivals, 38–39, 70–71, 75–77, 78–79, 81, 109
Casas, Bartolomé de las, 3

Catlett, Mary (later Newton), 11, 19, 24
Characteristicks (Shaftesbury), 11, 14
Charleston, South Carolina, 7, 17–18, 59; Emanuel African Methodist Episcopal church shootings and Pinckney funeral, 4–7, 72, 165; enslaved people in, 18, 59; Newton in, 7–8, 17, 18
Chicago: Dorsey's Chicago career, 112–14; Mahalia Jackson in, 116–18; as music hub, 107, 110
choral singing: in African American churches, 69; the Fisk Jubilee Singers, 67–68, 67*fig. See also* folk music and singing; hymns and hymn singing; music instruction and learning
Christian faith and worship: author's faith background, 4; Newton's preaching ambitions and Olney curacy, 24–27, 27*fig.*, 29, 32–33, 42; Newton's spiritual views, education, and struggles, 10, 11, 13–14, 15, 18, 20, 21–23, 24–25; slavery and, 2–3. *See also* African American Christian worship; American Christian worship; hymns and hymn singing; *specific denominations*
Christian Minstrel, The (hymnal), 55
Church of England, 4, 13; hymns and hymn singing in English worship, 4, 30–31, 46–47; Newton and, 25, 27
Civil Rights movement, 119–21, 122–27, 123*fig.*, 128; "Amazing Grace" associated with, 120, 121, 123, 125, 126; Black churches and, 122–23, 126; protest and freedom songs, 104–5, 106–7, 120, 123–24, 125, 126–27
Cleveland, James, 134
Clinton, Bill, 140
Clunie, Alexander, 22, 24, 27
Coal Miner's Daughter (film), 147
Coleman, Robert, 84

Founded in 1893,
UNIVERSITY OF CALIFORNIA PRESS
publishes bold, progressive books and journals
on topics in the arts, humanities, social sciences,
and natural sciences—with a focus on social
justice issues—that inspire thought and action
among readers worldwide.

The UC PRESS FOUNDATION
raises funds to uphold the press's vital role
as an independent, nonprofit publisher, and
receives philanthropic support from a wide
range of individuals and institutions—and from
committed readers like you. To learn more, visit
ucpress.edu/supportus.